Moo

ANDALUS

Moorish Songs of Love and Wine

Selected, introduced and translated by
T. J. GORTON

With a foreword by
JASON WEBSTER

ELAND • LONDON

All poems have been selected and translated by T. J. Gorton

This arrangement and translation © T. J. Gorton

Foreword © Jason Webster

ISBN 978 0 955010 58 3

First published in October 2007 by Eland Publishing Ltd,
61 Exmouth Market, London EC1R 4QL

Pages designed and typeset by Antony Gray
Cover Image: The Court of the Alhambra by
Mariano Fortuny y Marsal © Museo Figueres, Spain /
The Bridgeman Library
Printed and bound in Spain by GraphyCems, Navarra

Contents

Foreword

Moorish Spain has a special, almost folk-tale quality about it. Like the London of Shakespeare and *Merrie England*, the Baghdad of the *Thousand and One Nights*, or the Love Courts of Eleanor of Aquitaine, it has a rare appeal that captures the imagination and transports us to another world – a place of heroes and princesses, of golden palaces and epic battles, a land of silks and spices, poets and lovers. Moorish Spain – Andalus – exists as much within us as it does in any history book, or in some sun-scorched remains on the Spanish landscape. It can grab you in all manner of ways – a first sighting of the Alhambra, the scent of orange-blossom catching you unawares on a street in Seville, on hearing a legend or tale of El Cid, or perhaps as your eye falls on a passage in the pages of the book such as the one now in your hands. Once the connection has been made, it will stay with you for life, and form part of your dreams.

East and West alike share a fascination for this Golden Age: Arabs mourning a lost paradise, Europeans drawn by the advanced, exotic world that once lay on their doorstep. Both can draw inspiration here from a time when Christians, Jews and Muslims lived together for long periods in relative peace and harmony – a phenomenon the Spanish refer to as *Convivencia*.

This story-like quality in no way diminishes its importance, though, nor should it make it fall victim to the scholar's sneer: it is where its power – for good or bad – actually lies. Moorish Spain is perhaps more relevant to us today than it has ever been. It was a twisted, distorted dream – a nightmare – of Andalus that drove crazed bombers to destroy hundreds of lives on the Madrid trains in March 2004: their aim was to kick-start a reconquest of the Iberian peninsula for their perverted version of Islam. Such events might make us fear a 'romanticised' idea of the period, and rely instead on the historian's dry account. Yet the dream can work both ways: it is precisely within Moorish Spain itself that the lessons we need to learn for a better future between Islam and the West can be found. Culturally and religiously tolerant societies were created and then lost several times over back then. What worked and what didn't? How can harmony be achieved and then sustained?

I doubt very much whether the Madrid bombers had read the poetry presented in this book: the humour here alone would have acted as a barrier, not to mention the copious references to wine, and eroticism ('I caught her at the brink of sleep/ And brought her anklets up to join her earrings'.) Had they bothered to do so they would have caught a glimpse of a playful, fun-loving and inquisitive society. The vision of Andalus opened up for the reader in these pages is many worlds away from theirs, but in no way less powerful for it: dreams can lead us to destroy, but also to create; the choice is ours.

Here, in these poems – superbly translated by Ted Gorton – we can see the creative spark at work as two distinct cultures come together to create something new, something magical. Medieval Arabic poetry can sometimes seem formulaic, but in Spain, where Muslims rubbed shoulders with Christians and Jews, two new poetic forms were born – the *muwashshaha* and the *zajal*, which stand out from much of what was being produced at the time in the rest of the Arabic-speaking world: Moorish poems were often rounded off with ditties and refrains from the Romance language of the Christians living side-by-side with the Muslims – a kind of proto-Spanish and the earliest record of what eventually became the language of Spain. The connection with the classical past was never lost – witness the numerous references to places like Najd in central Arabia, unknown to most of the poets writing here but with a myth-like power to it almost like 'Arcadia' in the Western poetic tradition. Yet there was an openness and spirit of invention which allowed for exploration beyond the standard forms, the same spirit which made Andalus the intellectual and artistic powerhouse of the western Mediterranean: it's worth remembering that at that time all manner of Christians from the future Pope Sylvester II to the great translator Gerard of Cremona were making their way to Spain 'in search of knowledge'. But for their efforts, and the work of the many thinkers and writers of the three religions here in the Middle Ages, the European Renaissance might never have got off the ground.

These are the things that need to be stressed about Moorish Spain at a time of growing pessimism about future relations between East and West. There always have been clashes between the two, and probably will be more, but alongside all this existed a mutual understanding, trust and respect. We must hope that something of that can be recaptured today. In Andalus huge advances were made in everything from medicine to philosophy, astronomy and higher mathematics, and it gave us chess, oranges, paper, cotton and a fine tradition of love poetry that may – or may not, depending on the latest academic fashions – have influenced Europe's love-struck troubadours. What will future generations say that today's intense contact between the two communities has produced?

Moorish Spain is a jewel, but like all jewels in stories, it lies hidden, or protected. This book – like a key – may go some way towards helping to find it.

JASON WEBSTER
Valencia, 2007

The Poetry of the Arabs in Spain

The Arabs invaded what is now Spain and Portugal in 711 AD. Where there had been a somewhat dysfunctional Christian polity cobbled together by the Visigoths on the ruins of Roman Hispania, the Iberian Peninsula within three generations became an Arabic-speaking, majority Muslim state from the Mediterranean to the foothills of the Pyrenees. Scholars argue about exactly how fast the formerly Christian majority went over to Islam, and even more about why they did so: but by the mid-ninth century, the transformation was so complete that a prominent Christian citizen of Córdoba (Paulus Alvarus) could complain that the young men of his shrunken diocese could hardly write Latin, but spent their time composing all-too-secular odes in Classical Arabic.

The earliest poetry in this anthology was written before anyone in post-Roman Europe thought of writing in his own language, well before Beowulf or the equally rustic epic poems of the Franks, centuries before the graceful lyrics of the troubadours' first stylised love songs in the *langue d'oc*. By the year 1000 AD, Arabic poetry in Iberia was rivalling anything written in Baghdad. When the Mongols destroyed that capital and with it, Eastern Arab civilization, *al-Andalus* (the Arabic name for Iberia, derived from Vandal) carried the torch of the language, philosophy, science (especially medical) and arts of the Arabs, for the brief time remaining before their own civilisation was to be destroyed. It shone brightly in all these fields, but in poetry it reached the stars, and fortunately some of that poetry survived the new conquerors' destructive fervour.

Hispano-Arabic, or more mellifluously, Moorish poetry was neither indigenous, nor, at first, particularly innovative. The early lyrics have a provincial flavour, soon lessened by the arrival of accomplished singers and arbiters of fashion from Baghdad, like the famous Ziryab. By the second century after the conquest, poetry from al-Andalus was being imitated in the East and the Diwans (collected works) of its poets were copied and distributed, their poems recited and sung from Marrakesh to Palestine to Baghdad. New genres like the strophic *muwashshaha* ('girdled' one) arose, and a variant, the *zajal* or 'ditty', was written in the colloquial Arabic of the streets and the markets and taverns of Córdoba and Seville, with liberal spicing of local colour in the form of Romance words and refrains.

Poets in medieval al-Andalus followed their Eastern counterparts in their choice of poetic genre from the canonic menu, from *madh* (panygyric) to invective/satire (*hija'*), elegy (*ritha'*) to songs of wine and drunkenness (*khamriyyat*). The Iberians excelled in the love-poem (*ghazal*) and one genre they perfected, the flower-poem (*nawriyyat*), so appropriate for the gardens and orchards and verdant river-valleys of Spain. In all these genres, the basic formal and thematic structure of the qasida or ode was a given; mediocre poets compiled their verses from stock formulas, stringing together clichés like the image of the wind rippling the surface of water into chain-mail (which might strike the foreigner as original, the first dozen or so times he finds it . . .). This is not so different from what has been termed 'generic composition' in Classical Greek and Roman literature, or 'formulaic composition' in connection with epics, especially those thought to be orally composed. But in Muslim Spain as in the Classical world, a few great poets used the canon of genres, formulaic images and rhetorical devices as a discipline within which, subtly, through nuance rather than Romantic exuberance, they provided a delicate mirror of the world, of the human heart, of their own suffering and joy. And incidentally, of the momentous times they lived in.

Some of their personal stories are told in their verses: the brief love affair of Princess Wallada and the commoner Ibn Zaidun (slightly earlier than Abélard and Héloïse), so movingly captured in his long Nuniyya, and so devastatingly mocked in her short satires; or Al-Mu'tamid of Seville's lost throne and poignant poems from exile in the arid Atlas. There were a number of women who wrote poetry so good it won the grudging respect of the men who compiled the anthologies, and thus a few fragments of their poetry survive: I have collected several in the penultimate section of this book. Otherwise the order is neither chronological, nor geographical, nor thematic.

I have chosen for the most part poems inspired by love of one kind or another: tender, platonic love (Ibn Hazm), unabashed debauchery (Ibn Quzman), mystical love (Ibn 'Arabi and Shushtari), or the love of a father for his two sons, the love of a poet for a poetess cleverer than him by more than half, love for a lost paradise in Spain as the *Reconquista* bulldozed inexorably southwards. An elegiac flavour still informs the Arabs' image of al-Andalus: a Paradise on Earth, briefly found and enjoyed, only to be irretrievably lost. The spirit of place, the memory of lost splendour are preserved in their poetry, from its tentative beginnings to its heyday to its brilliant dying flourish: as more than one of their poets cribbed from the Quran, 'musky at the end'. I can only hope that a little bit of that splendour survives distortion in what must be the crude mirror of translation.

T. J. GORTON
London 2007

Note on two conventions of Arabic poetry
The reader will notice the recurrence of formulae like 'I would give my father for . . . '. This is shorthand for 'I would give my father as a hostage to ransom . . . ', meaning 'I hold . . . dearer than my father', which is to say, dearer than one can say. Then there is the gender thing. Most love-poetry is by convention written as though it is to or

about a beloved of the male gender; some is indeed about boys and men, as shown by the commonplace evocation of dismay at the first sprouting of a young man's beard. But some of this male-gendered verse is about females, as proved by inescapable anatomical references. So one just has to take a view. I have left it male in those where it seems really to refer to a male, and have more generally made it female, especially when the poet provides clues such as dress or anatomy. There are some other quirks that recur, but none that should cause serious confusion.

Note on the translation

I have grappled with the eternal dilemma: to rhyme or not? The originals are of course both rhymed and subject to the complex quantitative rhythms of Classical Arabic metrics. To rhyme their English versions, however, would at best produce English verse with an English rhythm, equivalent to the original only in that both rhyme in their respective languages. I have preferred to try to give the reader some idea of the sense and flow of the Arabic, of the cadence and especially the tone, when I could. That is daunting enough without striving towards an imitation of form that would be approximate at best and would necessarily distort the meaning.

T. J. GORTON was born in Texas and educated in Argentina, Turkey, France, Lebanon and finally Oxford, where he took a Doctorate in Arabic Literature. His first job was Lecturer in Arabic Studies at St Andrews, which he left for a temporary assignment in the international oil business, one that ended up lasting twenty-five years. He has published numerous articles on medieval poetry, mostly that of the Arabs in Spain, but also the Old Provençal troubadour lyric and its possible relation with Moorish poetry. He lives in London with his wife Andrée.

POETS

Ibn Sahl al-Isra'ili

Ibn Sahl was from a prominent Jewish family of Seville. He converted to Islam and drowned in the Guadalquivir around 1251. This poem is about the ungainly sprouting of a comely adolescent's beard, a commonplace image in Arabic poetry.

◆

Those tawny cheeks were so light and bright,
Until your beauty was blotted –
And you became like a candle whose wax has burned away,
Leaving only the blackened wick.

Abu al-Hasan

Abu al-Hasan lived in the twelfth century AD. This gymnastic image recurs in one of the *Kharjas* found at the end of this anthology.

The brightest night of all, I'd say, was when
The wine-cup never ceased its work;
I caught her at the brink of sleep,
And brought her anklets up to join her earrings

In the heat of battle, I recalled Suleima, and how I felt
                   the day we said goodbye;
I thought I saw her slender shape among the lances
                   thrusting at me,
And wanted to embrace them!

Ibn Baqi

From Córdoba, he was one of the most famous composers of strophic *muwashshahat*. He died around 1150 in Guadix (Granada).

Just look at Ahmad, untouchable in his glory
In the West he rose, what can the East do to match him?

Just as the night came trailing its dusky train
I poured her wine, perfumed with fennel and with musk,
And clasped her to me as the soldier girds his sword;
Her long hair fell on my shoulders like its harness.
When at last she fell asleep, leaning against my breast,
I gently moved her off me, undid her sweet embrace:
I feared my pounding heart would make a restless pillow.

My eyes may not be full of tears, but that should not
                                                    make them say:
'He has got over her', or worse, 'He never loved at all';
My sighing's proof enough of love, and doesn't everybody say,
'Listen to the turtle-dove, cooing for its love'?

Ibn Hani

Born around 935, he was accused of being a neo-Platonic
heretic and went into exile in Egypt, where he died around
973 AD.

◆

The night we shared was sent to us, a raven-haired harbinger,
We spent it watching the Gemini dangling like her earrings;
Our wine-steward spent it with us, and his faithful lamp
Lit up our night like morning, never faint nor flickering.
He sang as he poured, that waif so delicate
With his thick eyelashes hanging heavy,
Made even heavier by the wine.
His hands are fully occupied; he's bent down low
Under the heavy burden of the brimming wine-jugs.
They say 'He's like a slender reed upon a sandy dune';
Which shows how little they know of either reeds or dunes!
The wine's our only bed-clothes, and the dark night
Spreads itself to make a coverlet for us.
Full of passion, one heart to the other clings –
Two mouths find inspiration, and of each other drink.

Ibn Khafaja

Ibn Khafaja was born and died (in 1138)
at Alcira, near Valencia.

◆

Of all the local girls, I chose her as my queen –
reigning as she does between sun and happy moon;
You could read the *Sura of the Dawn* on her face,
So perfect, you'd follow it with the *Sura of Praise*.
I'm drawn to her in the morning, and then at night
A tryst with her distracts me from good works.
Her breasts all ready and waiting, pointed as a lance,
My kisses roam her cheeks like wild horses;
My desire grows as I pluck the daisies of her lips
And bend her supple body like a reed.
Like a tender branch she moves – but when
I start to harvest the fruit she promised me,
She pulls away from my embrace; I call her
From up close, but it seems so far away . . .
Proudly she moves, flouncing her dress
This way and that, like branches of myrtle.
But then as dawn begins to dissipate the night,
She comes to me, so appealing in her brocade robe,
Hardly able to contain her emotion, bursting forth
Like clear spring water from the rock.
She comes to me, more desirable than a hard journey's rest,
Long-delayed sleep, or calm after toil, welcome
Rain on the parched earth – or even today, from so far away,
Eternal Paradise here on earth.
Those nights, those nights when from one cup we'd

Trade sips of wine, our words like a gentle breeze
Swaying roses. The cup she handed me came scented
With musk, and in our sweet to and fro, as I drank
                                        from her hand,
The wine became pure light, transformed by my love.
I was carried away by her mouth – like daisies; her lily neck,
Eyelashes of narcissus and cheeks of rose, until
Finally, her body yielded to the heady wine's work;
Drowsy, she leaned against my arm, and with my kisses
I quenched my passion's fire in her
Cool lips. In my embrace, she slipped out of her
Embroidered robe like a sword from its sheath, and I
Held her, so smooth to the touch, so perfectly formed:
I said sweet things to her, this tender sapling on a virgin dune,
And covered her face like the sun as happiness dawns;
If it wasn't the sun, it was its sibling, related
As sandals are to leather.
My two hands went exploring,
One down towards her waist, the other at her breast;
One went down the Tihama road,
while the other went up to Nejd.
My kisses moved from her cheek
To her mouth, its liquor more enticing than any rose, as
My caresses roiled the whiteness of her alabaster cheeks.
I am garbed in such honourable robes, and of an age
That should rightly wilt at the sight of her youthfulness;
The full moon did all but envy me, of all men, that night –
But now we're far apart, and all I can kiss are the traces
Of myrtle she left behind, alone in the stark and
Desolate dawn. Oh, night of love, will you ever return?

Memories kept me sleepless, of a faraway, lost home,
Of the north wind, the scent of which I loved;
Then a lightning-flash split the night sky, and I told it
To greet for me those faint vestiges, and tell
Those who once lived there how much I love them –
No matter how far away, and no matter how unsure I am
They love me in return.
And do greet little Afra for me, and tell her to stop
Being the lost star of the North, and be a full moon to me!
For shall I ever press that supple body against mine,
Like a blossoming branch, and entwine her tight to me?
What hunter could capture such a fawn for me?
I would devour her with bites, drink her up with kisses –
Despite the fifty-one years between me and that young thing,
The years vanish when I see her in my dreams.
If only the bird of happiness would grant my wishes
She would be all that I could wish for, and
I would be fourteen again: *then* I wouldn't call her
'Little girl', nor would she call me 'Grampa'!

You're like a willow, when your long, thick tresses stir
And like a garden, redolent of perfume;
How many eyes have you filled with tears, how many
Throbbing hearts have flown towards you!
Your divine body is a tender sapling: in you mingle
The beauty of light with that of flowers.[1]
Your enchanting glance has snared me, languid, yet so
                                              beguiling –

Such a clever, deceitful one!
Is it an archer, from enchanted Babylon,
Firing bewitching glances at me?

His bow is none other than an eyebrow, arched –
With his eyelashes for arrows.
He wounds me with his every glance,
I looked at him and wounded him in return.
If you paint your pearls ruby-red,
I paint your beauty with flowers.
Your face alone, inspired with beauty,
Absolves all lovers from their vows.
Your cheek is like a parchment page,
Written on by your curls.
If a *dirham* were minted with your beauteous image on it,
The lover's eye would see a gold *dinar*![2]
It's as though precious musk wrote upon your cheeks
The refutation of those who know only how to blame!
He who burns with passion ardent as the wind,
Bow down to me, for mine is like a storm!
My body trembles like some great flowering tree,
Sending forth petals as its tears.
Whichever way you turn your face, whoever looks at you
Sees a *ka'ba* of beauty all around;[3]
I look at you through the eye of a magus,
Worshipping the fire in your cheeks.[4]

How many nights I spent, nights woven of your dark hair;
Like pure rain,
My tears fell down, and revived the bloom of your memory.
Following my tears as I wept, came the ruby of your cheeks,
The pearls of your smile.
I sobbed and choked upon a tear, blood-reddened
In the fire of your disdain –

As though it burst forth from the pomegranate-seed
                              of your breast.
Oh, those nights whose blackness I shattered, with the
Full moon of your forehead!
And I took my pleasure with that rare, well-hidden pearl!
So refreshing, the poppies of your cheeks,
So perfumed, the very air you breathe!
Swirling on all sides of your lily-neck came a dew of pearls,
With a froth of tear-drops running down the face
Of your wine-cup;
Overtaken by drunkenness, like a wind-bent branch reclined,
Your body arched and trembled, as though an ocean wave
Swelled up below and tossed your hips about.

She has the eyes of a gazelle, the neck of a doe, wine-dark lips
And teeth like pearls;
She drank the wine, and began to reel, in her gold-
                              embroidered gown,
As though the twinkling stars had caught the full moon in
                              their net.
Passion's hand bestowed upon us such a wondrous night,
                              wrapped
In each other's arms, like a cloak – until dawn's hand
Tore it and us apart.

The wood reveals the secrets of the garden, the river
Is its mouth, and the breeze its tongue.

I remember a night we spent together, falling drunk and
                                    amorous to bed –
The acacia granted us its shade, the bough gave the dove
                                    a pulpit;
The sun sank sickly in the West, while thunder groaned
                                    and clouds sprinkled.

I once saw a black man, swimming in a pool;
The water did not hide the white pebbles of its bed.
It looked just like the biggest, bluest eye,
With the black swimmer as its pupil!

Ibn Zuhr

Ibn Zuhr was born into a learned family of Seville, and died in 1200; he was an eminent physician known to the West as 'Abenzoar'.

◆

Leave your problem to Fate – that's kinder to the soul
And when the moon's bright face comes near,
Don't hold back, nor talk of cares, oh no!
Whatever has passed is dead and gone, your sadness
Cannot bring it back;
So greet the sun with the daughter of the vine,
From the hand of a delicate creature,
Smiling through a row of pearls!
Lightning flashed through them,
And the wine sparkled.
I'd do anything for such a slim and graceful fawn:
He drank of beauty, and now is drunk on it.
He took his distance, and left me with a broken heart;
Who can help me, distraught with desire,
Awash with tears when off he went, as though
Riding towards the pastures of Aqiq, taking horse
Among the tamarisks of old.
What do you say: when the midnight caravan set forth,
Cloaking the night in radiance: was it his light that shone,
Or did Joshua ride along with them?[5]

Ibn Jakha

A poet of the eleventh century AD.

◆

On the morning of our parting, we brought our horses to a halt
And the pang of separation brought me low;
I thought the litters bore full moons, with veils of woven gold,
And underneath the veils there crept a snake,
Seeking those cheeks of dewy rose.
They did not hurt those lovely cheeks, but
Sank their fangs into my anguished heart.

Abu 'Abd Allah Ibn al-Bain

Also of the eleventh century AD.

The spreading Earth is like a buxom young girl,
Cloaked in springtime, with flowers for her jewels.

The very air would seem enamoured of my love,
And so to waste away in pain and suffering.
Its woeful heart complains in lightning-bolts, and when
It weeps, its tears are drops of rain.
Capricious as she is, he must abase himself,
So weeping up above makes flowers smile down here.

Ibn Shuhaid

This poet and philosopher died in 1034 AD.

Quite drunk, she stretched full out and fell asleep,
And the Spy slept too!
As near to her I was, I moved up even closer
Like a friend with a favour to ask –
I crept upon her as sleep does, and mounted her like a sigh;
I kissed her white and tender throat,
And drank from her darkling lips,
And spent the night in ecstasy, till
The smiling dawn showed up.

The sword has in its heart a stream,
Where Death comes down to drink;
The lance's woody heart's a branch,
On which blood-watered fruits thrive.

Abu Hafs

A judge of Córdoba and Seville, who lived
during the twelfth century AD.

◆

They looked upon her eyes, and entered passion's trance –
Just as wine drinks up the drinker's mind!
Her glance puts fear into their hearts, while staying calm herself:
The hand that bears the sword has no cause to be afraid.
I lifted up my eyes to gaze at her, they wept
As do the clouds from underneath the sun.
When I recall her slender form, I moan with passion,
As does the turtle-dove upon a slender branch.
Her leaving casts a pall upon my heart,
Like the dark after the setting of the sun.

She has a rump, such a fine substantial rump!
That rump of hers tyrannises us both, her and me:
It disturbs me whenever I think of it,
And bothers her whenever she tries to stand up!

Ibn 'Abd Rabbihi

Court poet of the Umayyad Caliphs
of Córdoba, he died in 940 AD.

♦

I never saw nor did I hear of a pearl
That blushed for shame into red cornelian;
If you only gaze upon the beauty of his face,
You'd see your own sunk in ignominy.

Your new-growing beard has written on your cheek
Two faint lines, and now they've turned the town
Upside-down.
I had no idea your gaze was such a sword –
Until you went out garbed in those two downy lines.

She brings me my wine in her lovely little hand,
As fair and pink as the rosy wine itself;
When you see the pitcher bowing to the cup,
Down you kneel to pray, without ablutions first,
On silvery jasmine-flowers and golden daffodils –
All set on stems of deepest emerald.

Ibn Shakil

Ahmad bin Shakil was a poet of the
thirteenth century AD.

◆

They ask me, 'Can you love this gap-toothed one?'
I said, 'I choose a spring for itself, not for what others say;
Did you ever see pleasant water-moss
On a public water-trough?

Abu 'Amru bin Ghayyath

Ibn Ghayyath died in 1222.

◆

They said 'Your hair's gone grey!', and I said:
'So what? It's just dawn piercing through the darkness!'
It's no sign of ageing: when the bay stallion of love has run so much,
It must get dusty, and look more like a grey.

Ibn Abi Ruh

He was a notable of Algeciras (*al-Jazirat al-Khadhra* or
'Green Island') and lived during the twelfth century AD.

◆

Guide your mount to the Valley of Honey, and ask
About the night we spent there, braving the blamers' scorn.
I drained the wine from her mouth, and plucked the rose
                                                    of her shame
As we lay entwined like branches meeting
Over a stream;
And we exchanged cups of the finest northern wine.
Incense-smoke wafted from the garden, without fire
And our lantern was reflected in the river's coat of mail,
Like spear-points.
We lay there together until the cold morning drove us to part,
And only the nightingale's song could calm the turmoil
                                                    in my heart.

Ibn Faraj

Ibn Faraj died in 976 AD, and is the most famous
Andalusian exponent of the Platonic 'Udhri love'
said to have been practiced by the Arabian tribe of
Bani 'Udhr. This ranged from a mildly ascetic idea
of heterosexual love to an almost Albigensian
horror of the flesh.

◆

I have often shied away from a forward, willing girl,
And Satan was disobeyed.
She appeared in the night, in the blackest part of night,
And off came her veil:
But I managed to contain my intense desire,
And refrained from touching her,
as usual with me.
I lay near her like a young camel they have muzzled,
To keep him from his mother's milk;
In such a garden, one such as I can only gaze,
And smell the flowers:
For I'm no grazing beast to idly
Use a garden for a pasture!

Ibn 'Arabi

Ibn 'Arabi was a mystic and philosopher who lived in Murcia in the late twelfth/early thirteenth centuries AD. His *muwashshahat* are revered even today, and are devilishly difficult to understand, much less translate, as many images conceal oblique references to Quranic passages or incidents in the life of the Prophet Muhammad, and others are in Sufi code. The Arabic is so hypnotically – and untranslatably – mellifluous that his poems can be enjoyed for their music, and indeed Ibn 'Arabi's choice of the strophic *muwashshaha* form may indicate that they were originally set to music.

◆

With the dawn came a vision, so clearly revealed
Which commanded my faint heart to act

It was Love that summoned me –
But strength fled me, having heard
What happened to the Ninevites,
And I tasted their bitter drink.
Dreaming, I understood about Jonas – loyal but confused:
He missed the point, but guessed and
What he said was certainty itself.

By God, you who command my heart to see
What it yearns for, on its midnight journey,
For which it is the finest vessel –
You alone of all mortals could adorn yourself with
                            this well-guarded secret,
Fate and Destiny going 'round together,
Lost in the clarity of dawn.

Those two traitors[6] were condemned to the pyre
Which consumed them for their heresy. Wiser am I,
Though caught up in their flood, their fire a part of me;
Without sparks, the branches are safe from catching fire,
And rightly guide our meditations.

When he came asking for clothes and cloak,
He was whisked away by the Lord of the gift and call,
And came back victorious, a bright crown on his head –
One filled with pearls, like a crescent moon above
                                                    his brow;
Its blinding light a constant flash of rays.

The blind and sightless sea of darkness knows the
cloaked one,
And asks him wherefrom his inspiration springs;
The answer is, you said, chanting or reciting:
'If God dispenses His mercy through the world,
All differences dissolve, and the righteous come to
                                        Him in droves.'

Ibn Hazm

Ibn Hazm was born in Córdoba in 994 and died in 1063. He received the best education available during his time, which included religion, literature, medicine, history and logic. He was a prolific author; his best-known book is the *Ring of the Dove*, an epistle that has been called 'a rather nostalgic contemplation of the nature and experience of love',[7] and he has frequently been compared to Ovid. His poetry is cerebral as you might expect from one so erudite, sometimes reading like an essay on Neoplatonist theory; but is not without occasional charm.

◆

My love for you is without blemish,
While other men's is but a noon mirage.
I am all sincerity, my breast enshrines your love,
Its image and its text.
If anyone else than you inhabited my soul,
I'd wrench him out, rip his hide with my hands!
All I want from you is love and affection,
No more will I ask for.
But if I possessed it! All the world would not be worth
                                          an old camel,
The race of men a pinch of dust,
Nor all their nations a swarm of flies.[8]

The love I feel for you, by definition cannot end –
Nor can it ever change, growing less or even more;

It has no cause other than pure will,
And no-one knows of any cause but that.
If we find a thing caused only by itself,
Then we have found a thing eternal, without end;
But if we find its cause is otherness, its end
Will happen as soon as its other-cause is gone.

Have you come from the world of angels, or from this?
Tell me clearly now, for I'm perplexed and looking silly!
The shape looks human, except that if put my mind to it,
The substance it comprises is sublime.
Blessed be He who created beings so diverse;
But you alone are made of pure and natural light!
I know without a doubt that you are the kindred soul
Which had to bond with mine it so resembles;
I can find no logical proof of your existence,
Save only that I see you here before me!
And if my eye could not take in your being, I would say
You are pure Mind, authentic and sublime.

Ibn Zaidun

Ibn Zaidun was a minister in the palace of al-Mustakfi-billah, the last Umayyad Caliph of Córdoba; he fell in love with the Caliph's beautiful, headstrong and free-spirited daughter Wallada. His passion was requited for a while at least, and their love story is one of the most famous in all of Arabic culture. The flighty princess eventually tired of this importunate commoner, and his despair led him to compose a *qasida* or ode rhymed on the letter *nun*, the *Nuniyya*, that is considered one of the finest poems in the language. It pays homage to the standard figures of poetic rhetoric but despite this is never trite or formulaic, with the poet's pain and sincerity evident out in every verse. The rhyme is in '*ina*', both vowels long, with frequent internal rhyme reinforcing the plaintive chorus. All this is lost in translation, so I give a rather literal rendering which at least, I hope, gives an idea of the sense if not the music of this ode.

◆

Ode in the letter nun

Separation has dawned, replacing our closeness –
Distance, in the stead of our sweet meetings

Alas! The morning of parting has come;
Ruin bade us good day, while a messenger of death came to us

Who will tell those whose distance cloaked us in sadness
Fate cannot wear away, though us it wears away,

That Time, ever making us laugh in our togetherness,
Turned round to make us weep.

The enemies raged at our drinking from the cup of love,
Prayed that we might choke; and Fortune said: 'So be it!'

What joined our souls was sundered –
Severed, what our hands bound

There was a time we knew no fear of ever parting;
Today, we have no hope of meeting once again

I never gained favour with your enemies:
Would that I knew whether you have favoured mine!

I have espoused, since you, only faithfulness to you,
And have taken to no new religion

It's wrong that you gave consolation to eyes that envy me
Or joy to those who hate me

I had hoped that in Despair I could find solace,
But Despair has only stirred up my passion!

Our parting has parched my heart, yearning for you,
While my eyes are ever wet

When my thoughts call out softly to you, I nearly die of sadness,
And would do so, were I not so used to suffering

Having lost you, my days are lost in shadow,
While with you even my nights were white

When our harmony made life's horizon cloudless,
The spring meadows of Joy were made pure by our
                                        pure tenderness

And we pulled down to us the low-hanging, heavy-fruited
                                        branch of love
and plucked from it what we wished[9]

May your faithfulness be blest by spring-showers of happiness
For you were the very perfume of my soul

Don't think that separation from you will change me,
That could hardly change true lovers!

I swear my passions have yearned for no-one else but you,
Now have my desires ever sought a change.

Oh night-wandering lightning-flash, go at dawn to the palace,
And give a drink to one who gave me pure wine of purest love

And ask there: Do thoughts of me still trouble her,
As thoughts of her do me?

Oh East wind! Take my greetings to the one who would
Bring me to life, if she would but greet me from afar

For do I see Fate helpfully requiting us,
And not delaying our fulfilment?

Of kingly stock she is, as if God fashioned her of precious
Musk, and other men of clay

Or wrought her of purest silver, crowned with unalloyed
Gold, when he created and adorned her

When she stoops down, her pearls seem heavy, so
                                        pampered is she
And her anklets draw blood from her ankles' tender skin

The Sun was her sibling, when she was shaded in diaphanous
Cloth, though she's appeared but rarely to his rays!

As thought the stars' radiance were centred on her cheek
Like a good-luck charm, or an adornment

What harm if our rank is not the same –
In love there is enough honour to make us equal!

Oh garden![10] How often my gaze harvested your bounty of
Red and white roses, which the breeze exposed in full bloom

Oh life! I was fulfilled by your radiant flowering
Untold desires, all kinds of delights!

Ah, happiness, in which I went wrapped, cloaked in
Joy's embroidery, which I trailed along awhile

I don't mention your name, out of the respect and honour
I feel for you – besides, your high station makes that

                                        unnecessary

Though you are unique and have no equal in any quality,
I thought description adds clarity and precision

Immortal Paradise! We bartered your *Sidra* and sweet *Kawthar*,
For *Zaqqum* and *Ghislin*![11]

As if we had never spent a night, with only union making three,
Our joy making the Watcher's eyelids droop

Like two secrets in the dark night's heart
Until morning's tongue was about to disclose us

No wonder I thought of sadness, when caution forbade it,
While I let patience forget me

Indeed, I recited sorrow like a written *Sura*, the day
We parted, and took patience where I could

But I haven't strayed from the spring of your love,
Whose draughts only increase my thirst

I haven't disdained the beauteous horizon of which you are the
Star, forgetting, or hatefully avoiding

I didn't choose to leave you, and go away, but was
Compelled to go by Fate, against my will!

I grieve for you when drinking new-mixed wine
Or when I hear a singer's song:

The cups of wine hold for me no solace,
Nor the lute-strings any joy.

Be faithful to our promise, as long as I am – the high-born
Man deals justly, as he is dealt with!

For I haven't wished for any change from your company
Nor sought any substitute for your love

Were even the full moon inclined to love me from her
Dark abode up there, I wouldn't (pardon the expression!)
respond

Remain true: if you haven't been generous with your gifts,
I'll be content with dreams, memory will be enough

An answer can be a thing of great value, if by it
You restore the favours for which I still depend on you

I wish you God's blessing, while your love lasts –
Should you destroy that, you destroy me too!

How I remembered you in the gardens of *Zahra* –
The horizon was clear and the face of the Earth did glow.

The breeze died down towards evening, as though it
Pitied me, and languished from compassion

While the garden was smiling with its silvery water
As though you had loosened necklaces from above your breast

We amused ourselves with flowers that charm the eyes –
The dew trickled over them until their necks bent down

As though their eyes – when they saw my sleepless condition –
Wept for me, and the glistening tears ran down

A rose shone in its sunny bed
And made the moonlight brighter

A redolent water-lily floated by, embracing it
Like a sleeper Morning's glances had aroused

Everything stirred up memories in me, making me yearn for you,
And passion burst the confines of my breast

May God give no respite to a heart that remembered your image,
Sighed, and did not fly on the beating wings of yearning!

If the East Wind had desired to carry me with it, when
                                                    it passed,
It would have brought you a youth ravaged by his experience

Ah for those days, our bygone days of pleasure:
We passed the night like thieves, while Time slept

If only my desires had been fulfilled by our union,
That would have been the most precious of days!

My most precious and prized possession, beloved to my
Soul – if lovers can actually possess things –

Would not be recompense for the pure affection,
A field of togetherness where we ran free in times past

And now, I give thanks that I, at least, have been faithful
                                            to our promise;
You found consolation, while I remain your true lover.

How many nights did we spend, drinking finest wine,
Until the hand of morning started writing in the sky,
And the morning-stars began to beat upon the dark,
Chasing away the night-stars and defeating night itself?
But we had stolen greedily the sweetest of delights,
Without a false note intruding, of worry or of care.
If only those nights had lasted longer, so would my happiness –
But nights of love are destined not to last.

Drag on, old night, in her arms I'll never wish you short!
If my moon sleeps beside me, I'll pay no heed to yours;
But tell, me one thing, night, before you go: Is she faithful?
'No,' said the night, 'She betrayed you!'

Oh, you who severed the cord of my affection
And chained me to rejection, forgetting me,
Heedless of my endless suffering and woe:
If I treated you the way you treat me, you'd end up
Just like me, and I, well, I'd be just like you!

When will I be able to tell you how I feel?
Oh, my consolation and my torture!
When will my tongue take the place of these poems
I write to you?
God knows that it's because of you that I have come to this:
My food has no taste, the very wine I drink is flat.
You'd seduce a pious hermit, be a pretext for childishness –
You are the sun, eclipsed and veiled from my sight;
The full moon, shining through the slightest film of clouds,
Cannot compete with your face, luminous behind its veil.

Between us, if you'd only consent, there would be
Such a secret –
The last of all secrets ever to be revealed:
But instead you deny me your favour, something I could
                                        not do to you,
If my life depended on it!
Is it not enough, that you burdened my heart
With more than human hearts can bear?
Be haughty, I submit; put me off, I'm patient;
Exult, I grovel; turn your back, I follow –
Speak, I listen; command, I will obey.

May the rain-clouds grace the loved one's campsite
                                with their bounty [12]
And weave upon it a cloak of multicoloured beauty,
Crowning it with stars above its flowers.
How many statuesque maidens trailed their dresses there,
In the bloom of life, when Fate was their servant!
. . .

May rain-clouds of plenty shed their grace all around
                                                    the Alcazar,[13]

Amid cooing of the doves on every branch –
In beguiling Córdoba, home of all that's noble,
The land where youth sprouted like a lucky charm,
And where the noblest race of all sprang forth.

How many evenings, how many mornings have I spent there
Beside how many sweet gazelles, of luminous countenance?
The cups are proffered, their mouths fragrant as apples,
While the wine-stars seem to rise up out of them,
As we do rise before our superior, the wine!

Remember how we used to go down to the river-bank,
                                on the feast of the Prophet's Birthday?[14]
And took our wine from the hands of a bright and
                                                    beauteous boy?
Reclining all the while on a bed of flowers in full bloom,
Served by a sweet and dusky youth, so slender-waisted,
His mouth revealing perfect rows of perfect tiny teeth.

And how we took our joy, down in the Rusafa?[15]
 And strolled along, surrounded by an embroidery of daisies
While a gentle carnation-fragrant breeze came up to meet us.
When there appeared a rose, like a crimson-tinted cheek
If you held it to the light, the light would kneel in awe.
. . .
And how often did we gather at the Aqiq and its bridge,
Reclining among the red and yellow plants,
While a fawn gave us the finest wine to drink;
His slender waist sorely afflicted my body,
And his gaze, if he turned it towards me, wounded like arrows.

So tell this Time, its gentle grace long gone,
Its vestiges lamented, fraught with care:
How its gentle evening breeze felt such compassion,
And its starry sky shone upon the night-traveller –
Heart-sick with passion, I greet you from afar!

What would it hurt you to feel pity for me,
You who know so well what it is that torments me?
I congratulate you, oh my desire and my goal,
For staying so aloof from what I suffer from:
You laugh at love, while all I do is weep –
May God be our judge in what's between us!
Oh sleeper, for love of whom I sleep no more:
Give me too the gift of sleep, oh sleeper!

Love resides in the rising of these stars
And hopes are wafted towards us on the breeze[16]
Our love, so refined, hid us a while –
If only such happiness could last!
Desires that would not end before they've run their course,
And a time when our love-covenant drew no blame.
The pleasures we're allowed are sealed in musk,
And our union is wine mixed with holy water.[17]
The first-fruits of tender love are harvested when we're young
And intoxicated by the heady wine of bliss.[18]
How long it's been since my flighty love has fled,
Without fulfilling the pact of love we'd made.

The West Wind caressed me with its gentle breath[19]
And brought back memories of my youth, and such a pang!
While the lightning-bolt, whenever it flashed, never failed
To tease out a tear, then two, until they overflowed;
For can one so passion-racked control his tears at will?

Oh friends, if I grieve, well, the cause is plain to see:
And if I endure with patience, that's just the way I am –
Even if Fate has struck a mortal blow.
Today drink and play, tomorrow – business, as they say,
And the noblest men are generous, don't you know.

Cares have dumped upon my head all sorts of woe,
And the messengers of disaster never passed me by;
I spend my days tied up in hope's illusion,
Taking refuge in a night whose stars are slow –
The slowest traveller of all is the star that's watched by me.

Oh, beguiling Córdoba! Have you exhausted all desire?
Can a heart parched by separation from you ever quench
                                                    its thirst?
And will your glorious nights, once past, ever come again?
For you are beauty's image, the very sound of joy,
Prepared by God to be the sanctuary
At our mortal Earth's heart.

. . .

Shall I ever forget the joyful time we spent at al-'Uqab?
And the times we took our ease, ensconced in the Rusafa?
The abode within the Ja'fariya welcomed us,
And every desire our souls could have,
Of gardens and running water, was fulfilled:
It was a divine place in which to spend our youth!

. . .

I felt so sad, that even fresh-mixed wine gave me no comfort,
Nor did the slow melody of the lute-strings help.
I could not stifle my sighs, even when rebuked for them,
For nothing could console me since we parted –
Except receiving word from you, albeit from afar.

You used to praise the passage of the sweet and gentle days,
For the world was your delight, and spoiled you all too well;
You were protected from its cares and from its tiresome woes –
Even now the shadow of your presence, now long gone,
Fulfils the first-fruits of my desires, and gives me delight.

The Blind Poet of Tudela

This is another *muwashshaha*. The Blind Poet was born in Tudela just before its reconquest, moved to Seville where he achieved justified fame and died young. He is considered one of the greatest Hispano-Arabic lyrical poets. This famous piece is studded with internal rhyme and rhetorical flourishes which make it imminently musical in the original, devilishly hard to translate.

◆

Laughing through pearls
Beyond Time's reach
 Oh how I suffer
 She toyed with me,
 I say, 'How about it?',
Like a verdant willow branch
The West Wind and rain
 I can't live without you
 My patience is done:
 Betrayed by my hunger
When such a cup
How can Time stop
 I must hide my love
 Love's sun rises
 The sight of her
Oh how could a star
Light up her excuse –
 Can't I convince you?
 I'm wasting away
 I begged her, 'Perhaps.'

 Gliding like the moon
 Sheltered in my breast.
Worn down by woe –
Delicious tormentor:
'What "it"?' says she.
 She sways, as though
 Were flirting with her.
My heart's in your hand
Try as I may,
To gather your honey.
 Meets such a mouth,
 Passion fed by wine?
But it's too strong for me;
On my heart's horizon:
Hardly calms my passion.
 With its pearl-bright light
 And my plight.
Must I despair?
With tears and sighs
 But 'perhaps' made me sad.

Pouring tears, burning heart
Water and fire
Only joined by fateful events.
. . .

I'm bored with Seville, and Seville is bored with me;
If it could speak and write, as I do,
We'd have got on well enough;
My soul said, let's get out of here,
For water in the clouds is pure –
In the ditch it's dire.

Leave wealth to those who care about it,
For wealth is a battle-field of woe;
Throw off your robes of avarice and hope –
For the sword's cruel blade is not reserved
For the naked!

If my sacrifices meant anything to you, don't
                        heed those who blame me:
Do you remember all those nights we spent together:
You were not stingy with your favours –
But I was never satisfied.

Ibn Bajja

A famous composer of *muwashshahat* – and a philosopher, known to the West as Avempace. Born in Zaragoza, he fled the reconquista progressively southwards, and was reported to have been poisoned in Fez around 1139.

◆

Flounce your train for all it's worth
And drink until you're drunker than drunk!
Light your fire with a flame
Of silver chased in gold,
Topped by a string of ocean's jewels
Next to a beauty with dark eyes and shining lips
Whose cup is full of wine, that is
Water made solid, hot embers liquefied.
Behold, the light of dawn is glowing
The breeze wafts perfume from the garden;
Don't light a lantern in the darkness:
Put it aside, and mix the luminous wine instead.
The gentle raindrops' tears flow down:
See how the garden smiles, through the flowers?
The jewels of greatness have been strung
By the hand of a king, ornament to the monarchy
God has created no other king like him:
A bright full moon, fragrant as musk;
Compare him to the morning, to the
Generous sea, to life itself,
To Ali as he combats, or to valiant 'Amr.

What a lion he is, what a valiant predator!
What a lance is his, what a scimitar!
Stabbing chests, striking off heads!
Parrying, then thrusting through the day –
He swaddles his white sword
In a crimson cloak,
And lets his spear browse
In throats of enemies.
His countenance shines, though veiled[20]
Like a crescent moon through the clouds.
His standard flutters above his head –
Arabs chant, and so do Christians too:
May God fly the standard of victory
For the noblest of princes, Abu Bakr!

Ibn 'Ubada al-Qazzaz

A court poet serving al-Mu'tasim of Almería.

◆

I'd give my father for a gazelle from distant Hima, one
                                    guarded by a
Lion of the jungle
My creed is drinking the sweet liquor of Paradise,
From crimson lips
He enchants my heart every time he bends down,
From that waist of his
For he is shapely: he must descend from some fortunate
Line of Thabit lords.
Sleeping in the shadows as he does, under a canopy
Of drops of dew
He is languid in his coquetry, with those bright-red lips,
Ripe for sipping from
His scent is like finest perfume, his dress
Elegance itself
How he aggravates the passion of a grieving one who's sick,
Of an endless malady
Fond of pretexts, when distracted, he'd make a mute
Start to talk
Such a gazelle, a glance from him would heal
Beauty-blinded eyes –

He has inner light, and if you seek the outer bounds of love,
Look to him
He is both the water of Paradise, and the secret heart
                                                                        of thirst, if you
Drink from his spring
Behold Muhammad: walk with due solemnity,
In his presence
Like a new crescent moon, first appearing, he is impossible
To describe
Imagine purest water, generously dispensed: wouldn't
                                                                        that make
A saint recant?
A full moon, the midday sun, a sapling on a sand-dune,
                                                                        fragrant musk –
He's fuller, brighter, leafier, and
More fragrant!
It's not a crime to make eyes at him, but he who loves
Is frustrated
For fulfilment, as time goes by, is nothing else than
Hopes forlorn
It's a mirage, that has appeared, in the sighs of a
Dying man
My murderer you are, can you not spare the life of one
Heretic?
We used to be so close, what was it that happened, that turned
You away?
What's so wrong, you ask? Well, the army of Death itself
Has attacked
Don't enquire after a tormented one, wasting away

In silence,
Whether his hopes are fulfilled, since it depends
On a spiteful one
He's hard on me, harder than hard, but my passion
Resists all change
He contents me despite it all, though this despot has
                                        imposed love, not reason,
To govern minds
So I sang the following to him, and love can only be content
With such sayings:
   'This gazelle of Thabit has the very monopoly of beauty;
   If you're in love with him, you're bound to him forever.'

Ibn al-Hammara

Ibn al-Hammara, a twelfth century AD notable,
lived in Meknes and Granada.

Oh Zaynab, wife, if you have ridden far away,
Then I whom you left behind, will ride the same horse soon;
How could I desire another woman,
With you dead and turned to dust?
When they put you in the ground, I said
The very stars have lost their way –
Oh flower withered all too soon,
Could the heavens not have been generous,
Could the very breeze not stir?

The bird of sleep thought my eye was a nest fit for him;
But saw my lashes and trembled, fearing it was a snare.

Ibn Quzman

Abu Bakr Muhammad Ibn Quzman al Asghar ('Junior') was born around 1087 AD in Córdoba, and died in 1160. He did not invent, but certainly perfected the poetic form of the *zajal*, a strophic genre which stands out from all others in that it is written in the colloquial language (discussed in the Introduction to this volume). The thematic and emotional palette of his songs (for that is probably what they were) is all-encompassing, from ribald drinking songs with explicit sexual passages, to nostalgia for his lost youth, to long but hardly boring panegyrics to his patrons. He is certainly not a 'voice in the street' as he has been called, but is without doubt a remarkable poet whose delightful 'ditties' give us an irreplaceable window on twelfth-century Córdoba, an interesting time and place if ever there was one. He is a unique treasure, his verse is so musical one wants to dance, his point of view so fresh you can almost see him as he is described in his own or contemporaneous poetry: tall, blue-eyed, and . . . ugly! I have tried to give something of the colloquial, dance-tune flavour to the translations; these are not serious odes, but, again, 'ditties' and when they are suddenly, seriously lyrical, the effect – in the original – is powerful.

◆

Zajal 5

What I love: the taste of wine
And my beloved's kisses –
That blessed beverage
     Takes away my cares;

When you get drunk
You're coy – and then, you're yielding.
The wine grew old:
And now it's running out –
How sad I'll be
To say a last good-bye!

What would you say
About some Almoravid[21] joy?
If a moneyed minister
Found out about it,
He would hardly
Play that game:
You won't catch him
Outside of his own alley.

He hid dark intentions
Under his beauty;
And all wrapped-up,
Seemed purity itself:
Standing there
With unkempt hair
And henna-died
Halfway up his leg.

There's no *wazir*
Like Ibn 'Ubada;[22]
To see his face
Is to be his slave.
To sit around without
Praising him is foolish;
Happiness is
To kiss his girdle.

In far Iraq
        His generosity resounds
A thousand jeers
        To those who oppose him!
If his bounty
        Were brought to me,
The clouds would be
        At my command.[23]

Destiny
        Is his companion;
To pine for him
        Is bliss enough –
If you're afraid
        Of loving him
Just be steadfast,
        Obstacles dissolve.

I came to him
        In all sincerity:
'All I want
        Is your well-being;[24]
Don't – by heaven –
        Play the hypocrite:
The crow, you know,
        Died of that game.'

I'd give my life
        For bread and cakes[25]
And all the rest
        I could describe:
Wazir, as I
        Speak, my mouth

Is so dry –
        I cannot even spit.

The drunken man
        Finds true delight;
And as for me,
        I've found my way:
My heart is tied
        And shackled fast
And now I must
        Break free at last.

Zajal 10

Now do I yearn for you, Laleima,[26] little star
As one who loves and perishes for you;
If I die, it's all because of you.
If my heart could forget about you,
I wouldn't sit composing this little song!

I'm half-crazy, on the rocks;[27]
So sad, so full of woes!
See how long the day is, but
Hardly a morsel of it did I taste.

I said: my cares are such, as God is great!
I simply cannot bear it any more.
When I set out for the Green Mosque,
I end up way over at Little Elm Spring![28]

You are the ornament of every party,
Elegant, and well-brought-up;
If God made you a palsied beggar,
Such alms you'd collect – gemstones by the bushel!

Anyone who loves you is on fire,
For all the magic of Babel resides in you;
Every little word you say
is a priceless pearl of wisdom.

Two little breasts like apples,
Two little cheeks, white as flour;
Gems are her tiny teeth
And her little mouth, sugar itself.

If *you* banned people from holy fasting,
And said, 'Be heretics, one and all!'
There'd be no-one left in the mosque
Unless he be bound hand and foot!

You are sweeter than sweet fennel;
I am a slave and you my master,
O lord! And if any naysay it –
I'll pelt him smartly on the nape!

How long will you rebuff me
How long this meanness means to last?
Pray God to bundle us up tight
Alone in an empty house!

Zajal 11

Stuck without a drop of wine: now what could be worse than that?
God could find no torture worse for me, by Muhammad!

The world is what you see, try not to waste a minute;
Every day and every night should be a merry feast –
Indulge yourself while you can, before Death gets your number,
For don't you see how sad it is: you dead, and the world still living?

An hour without a drink: how graceless and how stale!
Or a day without some bawdy fun, or with no gay carousing?
I don't count pleasure pleasure, nor relaxation fun at all,
Unless I grip the wine-cup's lip with the wine between my own lips!

If you could see the wine-cups in my house, filling up with wine –
By God! If such a lover loved me, and such a wine could last!
Just come yourself and you will see Soraya,[29] making merry
With the wine-cup lifted high – I'll not forget the Pleiades
                                                    are above us.

Zajal 90

I fritter away my life in drink and debauchery;
Oh lucky me, to live such a wanton life!

Repentance for me would mean absurdity,
And life without drinking, a huge mistake.
'*Vino! Vino!*'[30] The hell with what they say!
To give up drunkenness would be sheer folly.

I'll free my servant, give away my wealth
The day I put aside the cup!
Bring me wine, in flask or jug alike:
I'll hold its gullet to mine and gulp.

Come on! Let's clink our cups together:
Tipsy? Drunk! Who cares for good behaviour?
If you want a morning quaff –
Wake me at the first *volcón*![31]

Take my money, spend it all on wine,
Divide up my clothes among the whores!
Tell me I am doing the right thing –
Up to now I never went astray.

And when I die, my wishes are as follows:
I'll sleep in the vineyard, among the vines
Covered in grape-leaves for a shroud,
And a turban of tendrils about my head.

Let the Devil[32] gather there all my friends,
And remember me for his sake, reclining or upright;
And if anyone eats a bunch of grapes,
Let him plant the stalk upon my grave.

I'll drink your good health from a king-size goblet,
While you turn yours up high, and drain it!
You graced me with such a splendid gift,
Your every wish is my command!

'Come on, let's have some fun with a woman;
We'll be a cunt ahead!' Says he:[33] 'it's filthy!'
'Well isn't it at least better than shit?' says I,
And the price is paid in full already!'

So here's us sitting around, when up comes this Berber girl
With a diadem in her hair, and such a lovely basket!
And not one made of thistles, by my life . . .
(Mind you don't come on too strong, she's not a
                                    bowl of porridge!)³⁴

'Milady', quoth I, 'of skin so white, what are you about?'
'I came to bed', says she, 'Capital!' says I;
To him I ordered, 'Rise'; he said 'You first!'
'Let's put some horns on her husband!'

No sooner had I laid eyes on that leg,
And those lovely, refined eyes of hers –
That my member stood up in my breeches like a tent-pole,
Making a pavilion of my robe.

And when I saw that creature all stretched out,
The chick wanted to burrow into its nest –
How could it fail to find it, such a furry one?
(here people will surely cry, 'For shame!')

And so, by God, I got down to work:
In he went, no sooner out again;
Pushing I was so sweetly, sweet as honey –
Until my soul gushed out, hot, between her legs.

Fine it was, but for the next day's insults,
Which led to quarrels and a fight:
'Unhand my beard, you ass!' says I,
'And you there, drop that frying-pan at once!'

One tears off an eyelid, another throws a punch,
While yet another rips clothes and bites;
Wherever I throw a wee green quince,
I get back a cudgel on my head.

These people are really not my sort:
When will this shameful scene be done?
As for me, by God and by as-Sahli,
I will not stoop to such a vile attack.

If they look upon you with the eye of scorn,
It's that this town isn't big enough for you!
Your skill is great, like that of Ibn Quzman,
No other's could hold a candle to it.

. . .

(The rest of this poem is a panegyric to a certain
Abu Ishaq as-Sahli)

Ode to a Radish

This little poem is not about love, but I could not resist
including it just to give an idea of the breadth of subject-
matter of these poems.

The radish is a splendid food, but the mouth
Of he who eats it seems to fart;
Its only fault is that it switches
One's anus from its place into the head.

My lover's house, now he is gone   Is sad and sere
Hopeless, desperate   I seek him there.

As one whose time has come, he left this land,
His home, so graceful once – a plain of desolation.
The mourning-dove laments him with its cooing:

Whose lover leaves him   No hope retains;
But only weeping   Love's remains.

Abandoned, far from him, I lie bewildered
Sooner could I reach the stars than bring him back!
Hear the mourning-dove, singing, as he does:

Oh Ban Quzman,   You weep in vain:
Stirring through ruins   Brings nought but pain.

Where is Ibn Zaidun's Lane, with its bustle?
Where the Mosque Quarter, and its beauty?
Burdened now with spite too great to bear.

Look close! You'll see a   Field to plow and seed;
The rest infested   Head-high with weed.

Those splendid parties – didn't I attend them,
With so many refined, convivial beauties?
And me all robed in exquisite finery –

Endlessly strumming,   Plucking of lutes;
From afar could be heard   Trilling of flutes.

Aban Quzman has reformed – bravo! (if it lasts);
His every day was a feast among days,
Midst drums and tambourines and dancing sleeves rolled up;

Now, it's to the minaret   Up and down,
Or genuflecting in his   Priestly gown.

The raven's ugly caw is loathsome;
How wretched he is, how ugly and how vile!
All we see is sadness – has he no hour of joy?

A curse upon ravens'   Foul sound and sight:
Birds of dire omen,   Black as the night.

Ibn Sa'id

◆

She came to me like the reddest rose
And when I left her, she was like a buttercup;
I stole from her the source of crimson shame –
I got what I wanted, and she got wet.

Shushtari

Abu-al Hasan Al-Shushtari was born in 1212 and lived most of his life in various parts of Al-Andalus, moving to Morocco and eventually Egypt, where he was buried in 1269. He is famous for having widened the subject-matter of the colloquial genre known as the *zajal* (see Introduction and biographical note on Ibn Quzman, above) to include mystical or Sufi themes. You might say he broadened the love-theme so dear to Andalusian poets to include mystical love as well as earthly passion. His poetry can almost be read as earthly love-songs, in fact; but the images are in fact Sufi symbols, and his wine is that of the Intoxicating Divine Love.

◆

Zajal

My beloved came to me, and did my bidding –
how sweet it was!
She forgave me all my sins –
let the gossips grumble!

Just as I despaired, she came, consented,
and sadness fled –
As the cups went round and round, we were as one,
my hopes fulfilled;
We drank, and the sinless wine
sweetened our breaths.
Fill my cup, for it holds my delight –

and you drink too, if you are wise!
My love is all the company I need:
light within my lamp, cling close to me!
Such divine nectar, such wine! And what a tavern,
with such music and such song!
In a garden whose flowers have opened,
whose buds have bloomed for us –
Where the very birds in the trees sing
sermons to our ears,
My cups and glasses are full,
but not with grape or raisin;
Companions, hear me well:
a wondrous time is mine!
How fine it is to drink such wine,
in such a joyous place!
Let me drink, and love my beloved
with every dawning day;
Only a fool would tell me to repent:
my path is the right one –
To those who blame me I repeat:
'a wondrous time is mine!'
I know about the past, and what's to come:
it's the doctor makes me sick!
In love I am the leader of my time,
the chief carouser!
I wasted my life making love to beauties,
exhausted all the arts.
In the dark of night, the full moon came to me,
unseen by any eye:
Such brilliant light flooded 'round my house,
I nearly lost my mind!
He quietly shared my quiet times,

and stayed with me when I moved;
I gave my soul religiously to the one
whom I adore.
His presence was in me and was my joy,
he lit up my hours;
I call him my sun, my full moon,
whenever we two meet:

'My beloved came to me, and did my bidding –
How sweet it was!
She forgave me all my sins – let the gossips grumble!'[36]

Al-Mu'tamid bin 'Abbad

Al-Mu'tamid was king of Seville during the 'Party Kings' period, and was dethroned and exiled by the North African (Almoravid) mercenaries he recruited to help stave off the *Reconquista*. He died in Aghmat, Morocco in 1095.

I spent the night beside the riverbank, close by her
Whose bracelets are as sinuous as the river.
She slipped out of her robe, delicate as a sapling –
Bliss it was to sunder the calyx from that flower!

She stood there, shielding my eyes from the sun's bright disk,
Shielded herself from Time's vicissitudes.
She knew she was as beautiful as the full moon –
And what can hide the sun, except the vagrant moon?

Every conqueror kisses this hand of his –
If it were less generous, I'd liken it to the Holy Stone!³⁷

Having parted from you, I felt bereft, in my passion
Like a soul banished from the Garden of Paradise.
I took my pen and tried to write, but only tears
Wrote my passion's story on the parchment of my cheek.
But for my exalted duty, I'd be with you right now,
And visit you as does the dew the petal of the rose.

From throne and pulpit, tears will flow
For a captive stranger, in a strange Western land;
Should he die there, his good name will be forgotten,
His joys will perish unseen.
Sharp swords and lances will all mourn for him,
Tears pouring around them like a flood.
To Zahi and Zahir, places he used to love, seekers
                                              of generosity
And largesse will come in vain, and weep for him;
For if they say his gracious nature died in Aghmat,
Well, *we* don't expect to rise again, once dead.
The crown was his companion, but that time's past –
Now he's cut off from all such royal things;
The noble sons of Ma' as-Sama' have been brought low,
Abased indeed are the sons of Ma' as-Sama'[38]
If Fate's sentence seems corrupt and wrong,
Since when do the just get just rewards?
All the weeping on their account does flood
Great oceans of tears over men's hearts.
Will I ever, ever spend another night between
A garden and a pool?
In a noble grove of ancestral olive-trees, amid
Cooing doves, and singing birds?
My lofty Zahir palace, refreshed by gentle rain,
And the other house opposite, we called the Pleiades –
While Zahi with its Dome of Happiness was jealous,
As is everyone whose love is deep and true.
As you can see, it's not easy, it's so hard to cope;
But to do everything God wills is, or should be, easy.

Ibn Al-Labbana

Ibn al-Labbana was court poet to al-Mu'tamid, and
died in exile in Majorca in 1113.

◆

The heavens weep, from evening rain-clouds and from

morning ones,
Upon the noble sires, the Banu 'Abbad –
Upon those mountains whose foundations are shattered,

mountains
That were as tent-pegs for the vaulted Earth.
The ripening flowers that covered the hills are faded,
And growing in the abyss of desolation –
A lair of serpents and lions, visited by calamity,
Like a *Ka'ba* hopes once attended, now abandoned by city

and desert folk alike.
Oh Guest, the hall where generosity once dwelt is now deserted,
So get yourself ready to depart, gather what you need for the road;
If you hoped to settle in their meadow – it's abandoned now,

its crops withered.
Traveller, the road you thought led to plenty was a deceitful one,
You had best change your course, for no guide can help you now.
Horseman, who once rode all those prancing steeds so

proudly harnessed,
You might as well put aside your weapons,
Throw away your mighty Mashraf-tempered sword, you've

ended up
In the jaws of a vicious lion.
When your time has come no weapon can avert it,

For Fate has fixed the time and place for all.
How many happy stars have sunk, how many pearls of
                                        glory scattered far!
If they have been deposed, well, so were the Abbasids
                                        before them,
As Seville has been destroyed, Baghdad was so before:
The one a light, snuffed out after blazing forth;
The other a flower, withered in the bloom.

They fought to defend their women, but once overwhelmed
Were led off, roped, in single file;
The grey stallions they rode gave way to the black sea,
                                        heaving like them,
Their every collared coat of mail was sundered, making collars
                                        for their necks.

Would that I could forget that sunrise, on the river,
With them on board the sailing-ships like corpses in a tomb.
The people thronged both river-banks, weeping at their pearls
                                        cast upon the foam;
Veils were down, no virgin hid her face, while faces and
                                        cloaks were torn;
Sundered were neighbours, families that grew together,
                                        and their children.
They all, men and women, cried out at the moment of farewell,
'I'll be your ransom!'
But away sailed the ships, with mourning in their wake,
Like the song of the caravan-leader to his camels.
How many tears flowed into the sea, how many hearts did
                                        those ships bear away!
Who could take your place for me, O sons of 'Abbad, if the
                                        very water of Heaven has gone dry?[39]

As Muslim Spain disintegrated, riven by fratricidal conflict and the ineluctable *Reconquista*, loyalty was in short supply; Ibn al-Labbana was a notable exception and remained faithful to his former master, visiting him several times in exile in Morocco. On one such occasion al-Mu'tamid was so touched he scraped together a little cash to offer the poet who had sung his glory and bewailed his downfall:

Take this pittance from the hand of a captive; if it contents you,
You will be the paradigm of gratitude.
So accept what should make the giver die of shame,
Even if the excuse for it is simple poverty.

The poet refused the money, explaining in a poem:

You see before you one well-used to faithfulness;
So leave my feelings for you nestled deep within my heart;
Even if you ripped off my clothes to reveal a traitor,
I'd sooner give up my religion, than my love for you!
I would fall into misfortune's trap,
If I behaved unjustly towards the prisoner;
I came to see you, not to seek any sort of gain –
May God preserve me from such a vile fate!
Even if great favours call for even greater thanks,
The virtue's with the giver, not the thanker!
. . .

Ibn al-Qutiyya

This 'son of the Gothic woman' was from Seville, a
notable and courtier of al-Mu'tadid bin 'Abbad (al-
Mu'tamid's father).

◆

Wrapped in a double cowl, as pretty as can be –
Reminding one of eyelids heavy with sleep;
Split it with a knife, it looks like the pupil of an eye,
Its eyesight sharpened by the blade itself.
But inside it looks more like a human ear,
Soft and wrinkled![40]

Drink at dawn together with the tender lily,
And pass the sunrise with myrtle and with blooming rose;
As though the heavens had suckled them at once,
Giving one white milk, the other crimson blood.
One challenges the sway of incense dear –
The other dares to rival the red carnelian.
One is like a statue, stripped to the public view
And the other like a lover's cheek, flushed by parting's pain;
Or if you prefer, one is like silver pipes, the other
Like embers which the wind has fanned to flame.

Hatim bin Said

The sun came close to the moon: wine, and a friend to
                                            drink it with!
Pass round the cups of fragrant wine, for joy is in the garden,
Where the breeze has flecked the river with a coat of mail, and
The hands of East and West have unsheathed their
                                            lightning-swords
Against the horizon –
While the weeping clouds do make the flowers laugh.

My master has taken power, and tyrannises me – if only
My tears had not betrayed my secret, I'd have hidden it forever;
But how can you hide, when your tears but fan the
                                            flames of love?
Have you ever seen embers floating on waves?
When someone blamed me for putting up with his
                                            tormenting me,
I sang this song: 'Blame me if you will, I'll always forgive him!'

Ibn az-Zaqqaq

Ibn az-Zaqqaq was from Murcia and was a nephew
of the poet Ibn Khafaja; he was famous for his
descriptions of nature, and died around 1135.

◆

My friends, it's not heresy to love your sons,
You two should know full well:
My heart is split, one half belongs to one,
The other, to his brother clings;
Small as they may be, my life is bigger for them,
And my good fortune's hardly scant.
Someone whispers, 'You secretly prefer Muhammad',
Yet another: 'It's Ibrahim you really love!'
Well, the father of two can sometimes be unfair,
But for me they are as alike as two drops of rain –
Unequal in years they may be, but not in the love
And fondness in my heart and breast.
Their rank is the same in the heart's roster,
Abu Bakr no less, no more than Abu Amr –
Time is sweet when I am by their side,
and Time would mean nothing were it not for them.
Any man wants to enjoy life, as do I:
But for me, there is no joy on Earth
But in their happiness.

Here's to a delicate creature, passing the wine-cups
as the morning starts to break,

While the garden grants us the pleasure of its anemones,
and the amber-scented myrtle;
I asked, 'Where are the daisies?' and was told,
'Lodged in the mouth of our gentle wine-steward!'
The lad denied it, insisted it was a lie –
But when he smiled the truth was plain to see.

Pass the cups here in the dew-damp meadow
As the morning's writ puts the night to flight;
The last stars have not set, but have just come down
From the skies, to glitter in our meadow!

It was perfect, when she came to call: we spent a
night of bliss,
In tight embrace until night gave way to day:
Her arms around my shoulders like a sword-belt,
My arms around her haunches like a girdle.

The wound in his fair cheek is no accident –
It's rather a sign, a portent unto us mortal men:
God sent it down so that we should clearly see
The way in which he split the moon back then.[41]

She sighed, and my passion's flames were fanned
By a waft of incense blowing on that fire.

Al-Rusafi al-Balansi

A famous nature-poet of Valencia,
who died in Málaga in 1177 AD.

They reproached me, blamed and castigated me, for
                                    loving one like him;
Debasing myself, they claim, by loving one who's base.
I said, well, if it were up to me to choose the one I love,
I'd surely choose another – but it's not!
I fell in love with his smile, his fragrant breath,
The sweetness of his lips, the enchantment of his eyes –
Such a fawn! He weaves his magic endlessly,
His fingers spinning thoughts of love into my very soul![42]
His hands play gaily with shuttle and with loom,
As the days that pass make sport of our fond hopes.
He clutches the warp in both his hands,
Holding the woof in place with his feet –
Tangled like an antelope caught in the huntsman's net.

He's an apprentice carpenter; I said it can only be
That turning wood has taught him to turn eyes and hearts!
Pity the tree he's cut down to saw, to carve and hammer on;
Just lumber now, and serves it right, for what it stole
From his coat and him, when it had branches still.

Ibn Zamrak

Ibn Zamrak has been called the 'Poet of the Alhambra', being the court poet of the builder of its earlier parts. While some of the inscriptions on the stucco and woodwork and fountains are incisively chosen passages from the Quran, many of the profane ones are by Ibn Zamrak. He is known for his stylised nature-poetry and for betraying and causing the death of his mentor Ibn al-Khatib; much of his work has been lost, perhaps literally in the smoke of Cardinal Cisneros' infamous bonfires of Arabic manuscripts. Ibn Zamrak was the only even remotely great Andalusian poet to actually see the completed palace, so his descriptions are very precious (though more poetical than photographic, as one would expect); that is why I have included two of his poems that evoke the Alhambra, as well as one or two of his highly conventional love-poems.[43] One great Spanish arabist (Emilio García Gómez) said that Hispano-Arabic poetry died with Ibn Zamrak, in a fitting way, 'on the walls'. So I end with a few excerpts from the verses on the walls of the Alhambra.

◆

Ask the horizon, adorned with brightest stars: for I confided
                                                    my state to him,
And made the languid breeze take a sacred oath to keep my secret;
Mortal souls are weak, you say, and weak as they may be,
The burden I've thrust upon them is heavier to bear than mountains.
My cares are so great, as great as is my passion,
That my suffering heart is tortured to the end.
He who follows an alluring glance down the road to passionate love,

Will have to reject all counsel and all blame;
For my heart and I have fled the realm of reason altogether,
The day that it submitted to the tyranny of her eyes;
For love is but a glance that infects you with passion,
An illness that baffles all the doctors with their drugs.
And strange it is, that a carefree wandering eye
Can lead the heart to such a grievous wound –
For it can't be for God's sake that a mortal, precious soul
Is brought low by love, from where it was!
Ah, when I was young, those moments that I spent
In exaltation at the joy of love fulfilled;
I took my loved one to a secret, lonely place,
Where no-one else could see us – but I shunned forbidden love;
On that day we could see the gazelles at play, and rekindled
A love from long, long ago.
I could not sober up from her glances' heady wine,
So bright, it lit up all the world as though it dawned anew.
She stripped away the sheath of clouds
From the sharpest lightning-polished Yemeni blades, and smiled:
Tears welled up in my eyes and ran like pearls down my clothes.
I found again her mouth, the one I was yearning to drink from,
But no! I could not forget that my love is chaste, 'Udhri,[44]
While my heart fluttered as did my whole being, as though
The lightning-flashes of Hima shared my passion.
That night, the full moon shared my bed,
And the eyes of the falling stars kept watch over me.
I drank pure sweetness and light from the spring
Of a mouth adorned with pearls,
Sipping its liquor laced with honey, and with it
Kissed a sea of ecstasy swimming with daisies.
Oh, the coolness of that mouth, how it quenched my
                                        burning thirst!

Oh, the heat of those sighs, how they caused my heart to melt!
Beauty's garden, ripe fruit for youth to pick
That willowy branch bent down heavy to me,
Ready for me to harvest.
I spent the night watering the roses of her cheeks, with my tears
Until the narcissus of her gaze had quite wilted by the dawn.
Other women tried to work their wiles upon my heart,
But what have their saucy hips to do with my pure love?
If only God could cause those days to come again,
As He sometimes renews His favours to gazelles of the plain.

She came to me in a dream, in a blessed, lonely place,
And her brightness soon dispelled the dark and gloomy night;
She travelled by night, with the breeze billowing her train,
And the heady scent of ambergris and aloe all around.
For desire is exquisite, but never quite as much,
As when it comes upon you just as you fall asleep!
We spent the night like two ghosts wrapped in languor, paralysed,
With no fear those evil spies could surprise us in the night!
Until the throes of morning woke the world,
And the breeze tugged at my garments with its gentle hands.
Oh you who ask to know the secret of my true love:
For me, that secret is death-in-life!
By God! I don't complain of passion nor of love,
Except to my beloved, preferring death, unrequited;
Oh, ornament of my heart, I'll be tormented always
Delighting in my affliction, in my passion and distress –
If I weep, my tears are naught but blood;
If I burn, there's no kindling but my very heart and soul!
I tremble as the lightning-flashes flicker, and kneel down
As the breezes reach us from the far-off desert hills.

The pennants of morning are unfurled,
Night's bell has tolled, it's time to travel on.
Go early to the garden, and drink a morning draught
Among the flowers glistening with the dew –
The doves have stirred from their lofty perches, and
Warble their sermons from acacia-branch pulpits:
In every sort of language, they coo in prose[45] and verse,
Each telling in his way of his own burning love.
The branch bends down, after the shower,
To drink from cups brimming with the dew,
While the clouds' tears spill out into the land,
And find their path through every garden.
The air, spreading joy on all sides,
Toys with the shining scimitar;
Rise! and share in soulful ecstasy,
Caught between flowers and pure light![46]
Be companion to the suns of morning,
With full moons swirling in our merry midst –
Wake up those drowsy drinkers with a drink
Of wine and lips' nectar mixed into a cup!
Such a lovely little hand, serving a golden
Wine like the sun at sweet twilight –
Let your soul find true relaxation
And comfort, its resting-place at last.
Do not disdain the wine of loving eyes,
Get drunk on it, and you'll find madness there.
But beware the arrows of those eyes,
For they are harbingers of direst death –
They almost brought me to distraction,
Showing no respect for anything at all.

Madly, I love a young girl, slender-waisted, wide of hips;
My body wastes away for love of her –
If chance would let me sleep with her,
I'd slake my thirst in the nectar of her lips:
I'd make a date to meet her in my dreams,
But how then could my eyes ever find sleep?
I'd lie awake through the longest night of all,
While you, Oh moon, are full as full can be.
I'll kiss the flowers inside their calyxes,
If your lips would but smile on them a while;
When you smile, you unveil a bed of daisies,
While your sweet saliva is the milk of Paradise –
Tell me, standing there in your embroidered sash,
Have I any hope of winning your love?

Oh, you who pine for Nejd, sighing for it all the time –
From now you can find your Nejd right in Granada's valley!
Stop on the Sabika[47] and take in that lofty Vega:
You'll see that hill's a noblewoman, unveiling herself to you.
Girdled with a river-sash, smiling flowers the jewels on her breast;
Narcissus-eyes, in full bloom, with dewdrop-tears in her eyes.
Lips parted, to reveal a smile of daisies,
Kissing the cheeks of roses all around;
At dawn, it seemed as though the flower-bed around her
Was a scattering of silver coins collected by the gentle breeze –
See how each tree has its river running close,
Each watering each, like friends pouring wine to friends.
So many full moons, harvesting stars as they go,
You'd think the stars came up to kiss their hands.
The pebbles of the stream are pearls, jewels worn by time

Until, melting, they swell the waters with their sparkle;
The Munajjim river[48] together with its flowers
Are like the starry sky, if you like a simile!
More beautiful than the Milky Way, its pearly bubbles
Are more than a match for all those stars.
The Sabika proudly wears a crown, which the glittering stars
Might well envy if they wanted ornament:
The Alhambra, may God keep and preserve it,
A ruby set atop the crown, and its glory.
For full moons are to crowned heads like so many jewels –
But well might they envy the Sabika's crown,
If they saw how star-brightly it outshone them!
Its towers put the Zodiac[49] to shame: for all its stars,
Its beauty has nothing to compare;
And these palaces, so elegant and stately,
Knock the paltry stars right down to earth.
His eye is godly, he who has been blessed
To see its graceful minarets at dawn,
As the delicate first rays of day gleam in the East
And set the stars to helter-skelter flight;
Off to the West they rush, as the dawn
Closes the eyelids of the night that they adorned.
Come at daybreak to the palace gardens, and see
The gentle branches swaying with unrequited love
For the trees will never dance with joy
Unless they hear the warbling of the prince of birds –
When the doves begin to sing
Their subtle magic tunes, following the singer's lead.
Granada! May God the Merciful give joy to those
Who dwell there, with their songs of secret joys;
Her gentle breeze has put their souls in sweet captivity.
May God grant them endless days of happiness,

With warm and golden gatherings and bright and joyful nights,
And if ever drought makes her orchards dry and barren,
May He restore their life with ever-flowing water of fertility.

Oh, God! How beautiful is the garden of youth –
Before the flowers of old age crop up!
When I was young, I drank deep from the cup of love's
Wine, its pearly bubbles on my beloved's lips;
Her beauty was such, the full moon would blush
When she took off her veil.
Her graceful form put the tender bough to shame,
Grace no earthly bough could match!
Her glance shone bright as a new sword
And bewitched my soul with the magic of her eyes.
Whenever she removed her veil, I thought I saw
The sun: but this is one that never sets.
And when at last I could gaze on her at length,
I turned away my eyes, fearing the evil spy.
Do you think I have a good excuse, if my heart burns
When he lightning flashes, or the sad wind sighs,
And flies off on the amorous breeze
When the wind gives its wings a lift?
Is it criminal to yearn passionately for love,
When the yearning one is spurred by youth?
Passion has set a fire within his breast, and now
That fire has burnt the throbbing heart within.
His eyes are pregnant rain-clouds
That have poured their flood upon his cheeks.

Granada! Ever the home of peace and fondest hope,

Just being there is both desire and satisfaction;
Had I but found that for myself, I would not
Have suffered all those long and sleepless nights.
But soon, it shall be granted blessed peace once more,
When he who has been absent comes back home at last.
The people will praise his triumphs, the poets
Will celebrate them in glory-matching verse –
And may this motto be written over every door:
'With the aid of God, victory is near!'

Granada's breeze is languid, but cures the languishing;
Its gardens are verdant, with well-watered flowers all around,
Water enough to quench a fiery thirst.
An early cloud floated over its hills
And sent a shower down to the prayer-place.
Whenever its eyelids tried to open,
You see the flowers smiling in their leafy beds.
The garden showed off its rare beauty,
And the river like a sword stripped of its scabbard.
The spreading trees give shade so dark and private
It's the perfect place to take a noonday nap!
When the lightning flashes against the vaulted sky,
It seems to play about with polished swords.
She is a noble lady, the Sabika is her crown;
From the lofty tower's turret, she looks down,
As though she were a queen reigning over it,
With the Generalife garden as her throne.
. . .

From the Alhambra – Patio of the Myrtles

Blessed is He who entrusted dominion to you
And gave Islam, through you, preference and favour;
For how many towns of Unbelievers did you visit in the morning,
By evening being master of their lives!
You yoked their captive necks, and they became
The slaves who toil to build your palace walls;
You vanquished Algeciras by the sword, valiantly,
Forcing open a door that had been closed to victory,
And along with it you conquered twenty other forts
Whose booty you distributed to your army –
If Islam had its choice of any wish, it would wish
For nothing else than your safety and long life!

. . .

From the Alhambra – Court of the Two sisters

I am the garden that adorns Beauty itself
Look at my beauty and you'll know my noble rank!

. . .

The five Pleiades take refuge here by night,
Where the gentle Zephyr rises to greet the dawn;
My luminous dome has no equal on this earth,
Replete with grace and charms, both hidden and revealed.

. . .

From the Alhambra – Mirador of Lindaraxa

My charms are so beguiling that the very stars
In the Heavens strive to mimic me.
I am the shining eye[50] of this garden,
And the pupil of the garden is our lord Muhammad!

. . .

Ibn Zakur

Ibn Zakur lived much later than the Andalusian poets in
this anthology; he was from North Africa, born in Fez and
died in Algiers in the eighteenth century. I have included
one poem by him to show how the wine-and-love poetry in
the Andalusian style survived (at least in its conventional
images) well after the 'final solution'.

◆

Pass round the cups

Pass round the cups of crimson-lipped wine
　　　And Oh! What a wine, to rival the
　　　　　　pomegranate-blossom;
Cleanse my soul with the wine you pour,
　　　Perhaps I'll find relief for my feverish thirst.
I'd sell my father for such a fawn, one that
　　　Shot me with eyelash-feathered arrows, right
　　　　　　through the heart,
The grieving, bewildered heart he tore with his glance
　　　Like an unsheathed sword.
A mole of ambergris, musky at the end – the pearls he strung
　　　Pass all understanding.
His radiance, patterned on the dawn, or the full moon's light
　　　Distracted me with passion.
His lips parted, to reveal a shining firebrand
　　　That kindled a raging blaze.
Narcissus in his gaze, roses in his cheeks;
　　　Hearts' blood to shame the anemone.

Beauteous moon over a pliant silvery bough,
    Twin of the *ban*-tree.
He drew against me the sword of his two eyes, and
    My arms were helpless, the fire raged within.
    Desire for this gazelle in human form wore me out,
    My reason faltered when I saw him go away.
    My eyes rained forth tears, my love revealed
    That which no veil could hide.

WOMEN POETS

◆

There were women in Muslim Spain who wrote poetry that was acknowledged by male poets and anthologists to be as good as any; but things being what they were, none of them had the good fortune to have her works collected in a *Diwan* (Complete Collected Poems of one poet). As with Sappho, for instance, we must glean an idea of their work from fragments cited in general anthologies; as often as not, they appear as isolated verses illustrating some anecdote, often about a male poet. Because of this fragmentary situation, I have grouped their verses together in this section.[51] Their poetry is less riddled with formulae ('smiling through daisies', 'stripped like a sword', etc.) than male poetry.

Hafsa bint Hamdun

Hafsa bint Hamdun was from Guadalajara and
lived in the tenth century AD.

I miss my lover so, and yearn for him night and day –
But Oh! The night he went away,
What a frightful night, what a night!

I have a lover, who's stubborn as can be;
He never gives a single inch, even if I walk out;
He said, 'Have you ever seen another man like me?'
So I said, 'So who could compare with me?'

Don't you feel a pang, when you hear: 'It's time to
                                          leave, it's time!'
This cruel separation's more than I can bear!
With him gone, there's nothing left but death,
Or a life that's just a harvest of sorrows.
I gave myself to him, and life in the shadow of our love
Was exquisite, a garden of lush delights.
Oh nights of happiness, without a reproachful word,
United, untroubled by disdain –
Now he's gone! If only I could know
If he'll ever come back, and be as once he was!

Wallada bint al-Mustakfi-billah

Wallada bint al-Mustakfi-billah was the daughter of the last Omayyad Caliph of Córdoba, and lived there during the eleventh century. She was an intelligent, fiery, free-spirited and reportedly free-loving beauty, and inspired some of the best love-poetry to come out of Al-Andalus, that of Ibn Zaidun. Unfortunately much of what survives of her own work consists of fragments of scathing satire aimed at her former lover, who is described in crude terms that hardly seem compatible with the restrained and beautiful verse of his long love-poem (the '*Nuniyya*'). She never married and died in 1091.

Wait for me, I'll come to you as soon as darkness falls;
Our secret will be safer in the night –
For if the sun saw us together,
It would not shine, the moon would fail to rise,
And the stars would stick immobile in their tracks.

❖

Now that we've separated, what hope is there for us?
What can lovers complain of – *suffering*?
Oh, our times together, that winter, I lay
There as on embers, burning with passion;
Now I lie here alone, forsaken, for Fate
Made haste to bring about that which I feared.
The nights come and go, and this separation

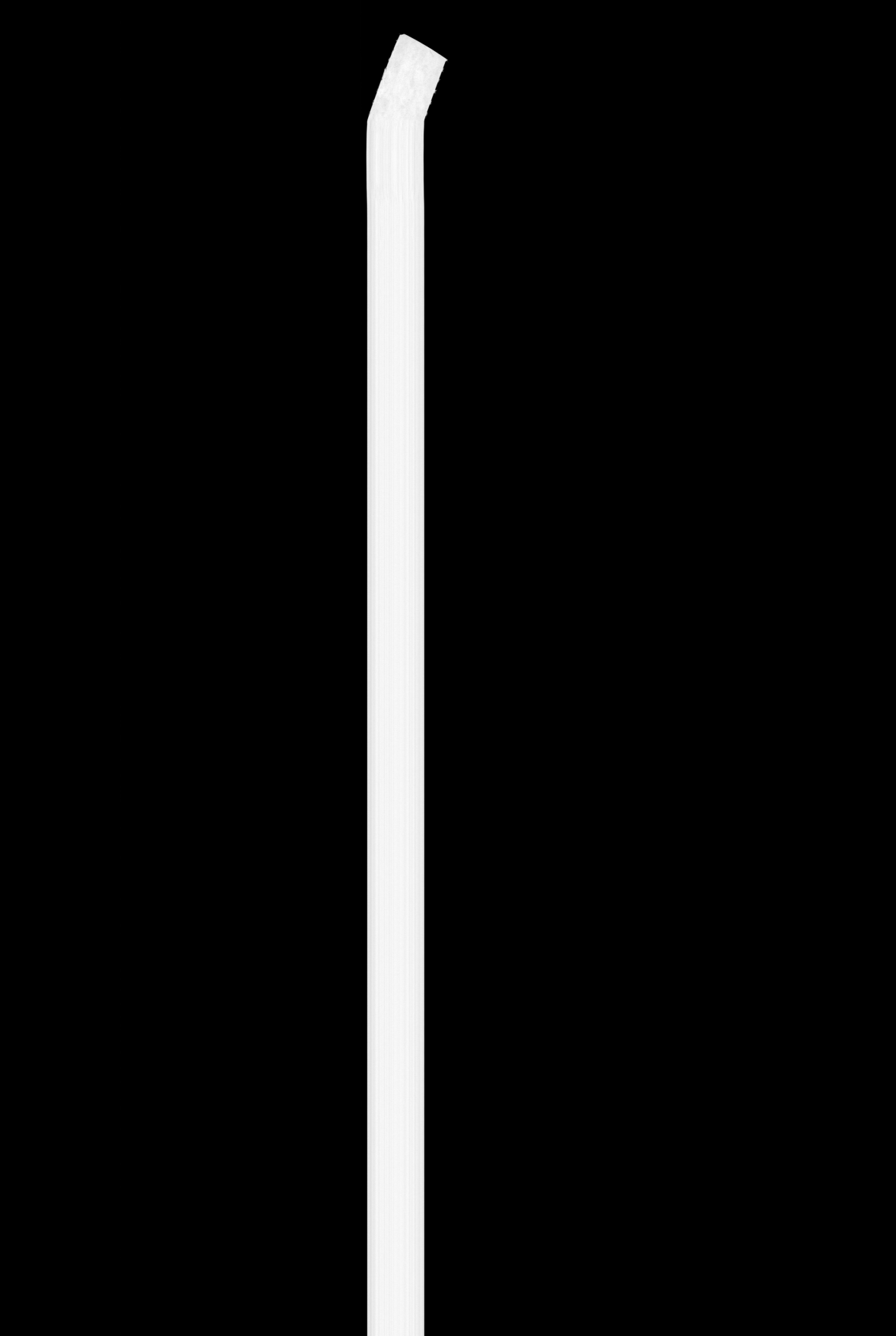

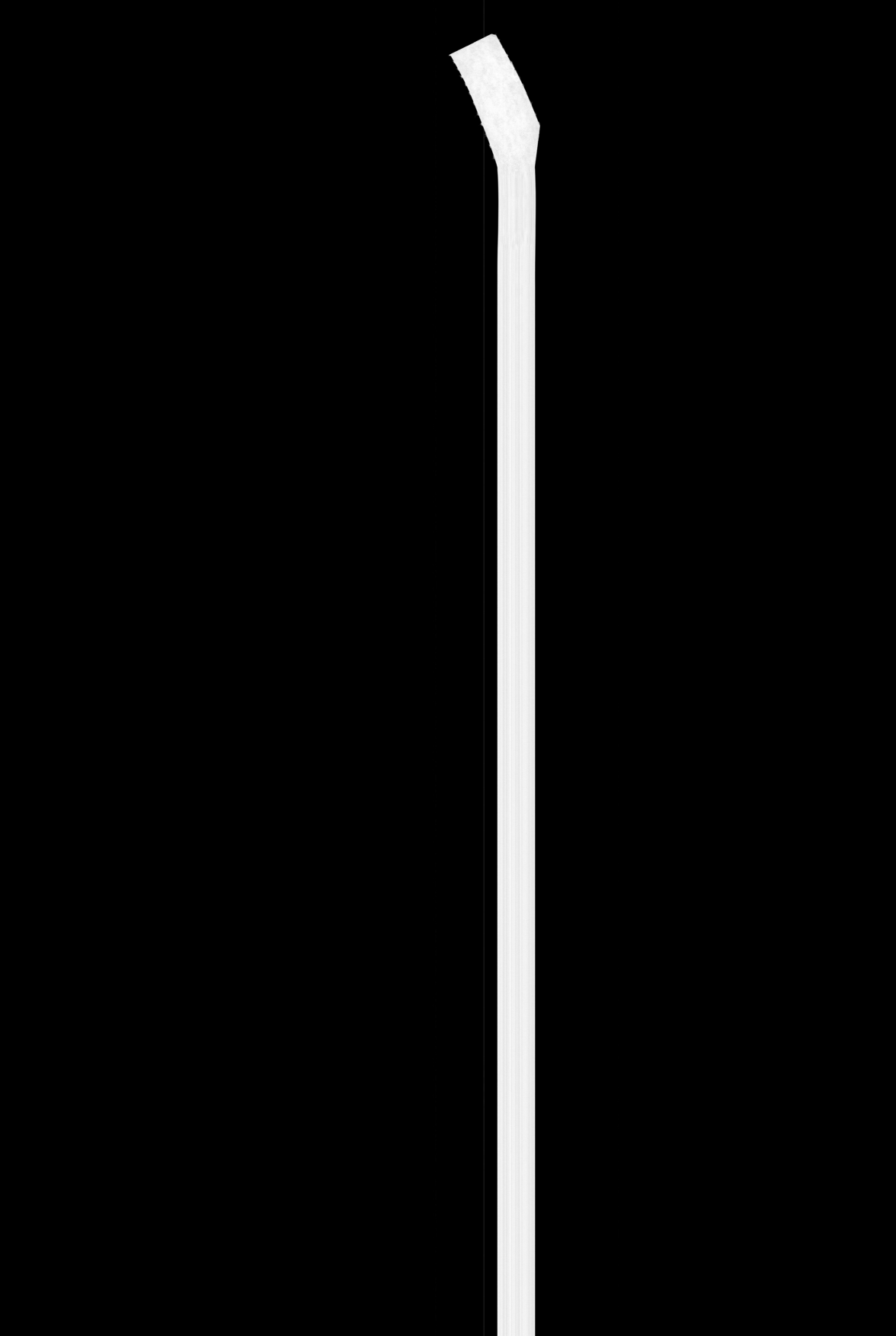

Seems to have no end. Patience has no power
To free me from the bonds of my desire.
May God reward the land you've settled in
With plentiful life-giving showers and floods of joy

Ibn Zaidun, famous as he may be,
Is in love with trouser-legs!
When he sees the penis of a date-palm,[52]
He flies to it like the swiftest bird around.

He's known as the Hexagon, and that's a name
He'll never shake, though he shake off life itself!
Queer, sodomite, fornicator, pimp, cuckold and thief!

Ibn Zaidun, famous as he may be, reproaches me –
                              blameless as I am!
Every time we pass each other, he glares malignantly at me,
As though I was about to geld the holy Caliph Ali!

Muhya bint al-Tayyani

Muhya bint al-Tayyani was one of the women who attended Wallada's salon-like court of free-spirited women. Her name may indicate that she was the daughter of a fig-seller, and did seem to have a thing about fruit (and male genitalia).

> Oh Wallada! Your secret's out, your baby's born,
> with never a husband in sight!
> You're like the Virgin Mary, but instead of a palm-tree,
> You've leaned upon an erect penis![53]

> You who treat your friends with gifts of peaches,
> Welcome!
> For they refresh the body when it's hot.
> They look like young girls' breasts with their roundness,
> But put the heads of penises to shame!

Nazhun bint al-Qila'i

Nazhun bint al-Qila'i was from Granada and lived during the twelfth century AD, though neither her precise dates nor any other facts are known for sure about her. One legend has her mocking Ibn Quzman for his alleged ugliness, while another says he did enjoy her favours at least once.

◆

Nazhun was famous for her ability to improvise apt verses on the spot, a talent much appreciated by the Arabs to this day. Here are two examples:

One poet challenged another, who was blind, to complete the following verse:

'If only you had eyes to see with whom you speak.'

There was a long pause, and he was unable to think of anything; but Nazhun shot back:

You'd be struck dumb by the sight of her anklets,
With the full moon rising from her gown –
Enclosing in its folds a slender bough.

When Abu Sa'id (Governor of Granada) was courting her he wrote this to her:

Oh, you who have a thousand lovers, and loved ones;
It seems to me you are too free and easy with your charms.

She answered:

Oh Abu Bakr, you occupy a place I refuse to all others;
Could any but my true love dwell within my breast?
If I feel love for other men,
All pious Muslims know that Abu Bakr has divine priority.[54]

All nights, by God, are fair enough,
But Sunday is the fairest of them all:
If only you could have seen us,
When the Watcher fell asleep –
You'd have seen no-one but the noonday Sun
In the full Moon's arms, or a frail gazelle
In a lion's strong embrace.

Who will rid me of this stupid suitor,
With his insolent gestures and rude behaviour?
He wants me to make love! even if he wanted a slap,
I would refuse: his wretched head should be hidden in a bag,
His ugly face covered with a mask.

I'd give my father for the one who leaves me weak,
The black-eyed one
He passed by with a throng of his admirers,
Picking flowers
He recited for them some verses of his own,
Deserving of reward
After he reminded me of his love for me, in another
Verse of his

If he wanted, he could have kept his peace, and left
Me undisturbed
Instead he wrenched my heart and put it on the fire
Wretched me!
He goes on stirring up this passion
With his song
If a maiden wants a reasonable man, she needs to
Play hard to get!
He loves her, but puts on a haughty act
And so she sings:
'He desires me, if he does not see me,
He desires me!
But if he sees me, he turns and saunters off, as though
He didn't even see me!'[55]

Hafsa bint al-Hajj 'Ar-Rakuniyya'

Hafsa bint al-Hajj 'Ar-Rakuniyya' came from the Alpujarras hills near Granada, and lived in the twelfth century AD (d. 1190). Her poetry is justly famous, which makes it all the more to be regretted that so little of it has survived. She had an eventful life during a chaotic time in the history of Al-Andalus, loving a poet (Abu Ja'far) who was killed by another suitor, the jealous (and powerful) governor of Granada, Abu Sa'id. She dared to enshrine her grief at her lover's death in a famous poem, and then went herself into prudent exile in Marrakesh where she lived by being tutor to the royal princesses.

◆

Hafsa's poet-lover Abu Ja'far wrote an indiscreet poem about their tryst in a poplar-grove by a river-bank, in which he wallowed in Romantic images:

> God preserve forever the night we escaped from those who
> blame us,
> The evening we hid in Mu'ammal's poplar-grove;
> The perfume in the air about us seemed to come from Najd,
> Brought by a clove-perfumed breeze all the way here.
> In an acacia, a turtle-dove warbled just for us
> And a bough of basil bent down to the stream;
> You could see the meadow taking joy in what we showed it:
> Embracing, uniting, and mutual ecstasy.

Hafsa answered him with the following, the ultimate deflation of the pathetic fallacy:

I swear (by your life), the meadow never smiled at our embrace,
It rather scowled in envy and bitter jealousy!
The river didn't murmur in delight to see us close,
Nor did the dove sing of our love, but his own.
You'd do better to refrain from noble gushing –
For a prophet's never welcome close to home;
And the horizon only revealed its stars above
So that they can the better spy on us.

So you think you are the world's best judge of beauty,
And of all things amorous?
I received your poem, all right, but that doesn't mean
I agree with what you say.
Oh pretentious one! Don't you know a lover's despair
Only tightens the reins he's held by?
You have gone quite astray, and have quite failed
To lead me anywhere at all.
You have always thought of safety when you ran a race,
Until you tripped, and garnered only shame
And vile ignominy.
By God I swear the rain-clouds bring
Their eternal bounty to the earth,
And flowers are always safe within their calyx.
If you only knew my excuse, you'd leave off blaming me,
And stop this endless litany of reproach.

You were once the most elegant of men
Until Fate brought you low:
You had to fall in love with a lady black as night,

And now your beauty wears a shroud, in mourning, as it were.
No joy can shine out from those dark recesses, can it?
And you'd hardly say that she was shy to boot.
By God! You are the smartest one who ever
Fell in love, so tell me: who could ever love a heart
Without a ray of light, where no single bud could bloom?

Oh horseman, riding like the wind:
Slow down a while, and let me tell
A thing or two of what I feel for you.
No-one has ever felt the torment that I feel;
All I ask is that you're satisfied – my only joy
Is seeing you happy, and affectionate with me –
And so I'll strive, until the end of time.

When a suitor importuned her, Hafsa improvised:

I beg you to entrust to me a parchment
To shield me against the vicissitudes of Fate;
With your right hand, write these words on it:
Praise God – and praise no-one else but Him!

Hamda bint Ziyad

Hamda was from Wadi Esh and lived
during the twelfth century AD.

My tears disclosed my secrets by the river, for its beauty;
A river overflowing into every meadow,
And a meadow encroaching on every river.
Among all the gazelles there was one fawn made for love,
It seized my mind, and stole away my heart;
When its gaze gets sleepy, it's for a reason –
And that very reason banished sleep from me.
When they loosened their long hair,
I saw the full moon rising from the night horizon,
As though the dawn's twin brother had died,
And out of sadness cloaked itself in mourning.[56]

The gossips did their best to come between us,
And neither you nor I could find a way to beat them;
They launched a bitter war against our reputations –
On my side were very few who would defend me.
And so I attacked them with your eyes and with my tears,
And – from my soul – with sword and flood and fire!

Qasmuna bint Ismail

Qasmuna bint Ismail was already a *rara avis*, being a woman poet some of whose work has survived; but she was also a Jewish woman poet living in the court of the Muslim king of Granada, where her father, a famous eleventh-century poet named Samuel Ha-Nagid bin Nagrilah, was counsellor (*wazir*); unlike most Andalusian Jewish poets including her father, she wrote in Arabic. Her verse has been said to contain Biblical reminiscences, and it certainly has a nostalgic charm.

◆

I can see a garden, with ripe fruit to be picked;
But no gardener lays a hand on it.
Woe is me! My youth is wasting fast, and I am
Left alone with nothing but what I cannot name.

THE KHARJAS

◆

Al-Andalus produced at least one unique poetic genre, one that is not a genre at all: the *kharja*, the 'exit' or last refrain of a *muwashshaha* (the strophic form that originated in Al-Andalus). The *kharjas* are mostly in a mixture of colloquial Arabic and the spoken Romance dialect of the day, and are (along with the Romance passages in Ibn Quzman's *zajals*) a unique source of our knowledge of that dialect from a time when it was simply never written down. Depending on your point of view, they represent either (1) a fragmentary remnant of Romance poetry from a Christian-Latin tradition supposed to exist in Iberia before the Arabic invasion; or (2) bits of poetry borrowed from popular songs, or simply fabricated by the Andalusian Arab authors of *muwashshahas* to provide a 'spicy' ending for their verses. The fact that even the Romance *kharjas* conform to a version of Classical Arabic metre, along with the rest of the *muwashshaha* which they close, would seem to support hypothesis (2) above, as would the fact that we have no serious evidence for (1).

Be that as it may, the fifty or sixty known extant *kharjas* are delightful, sometimes bawdy, often put (presumably by male poets) in the mouths of women. Many of them are obscure, and all are difficult to decipher and have caused endless squabbles among scholars, not surprising given that these refrains have

come down to us through a manuscript tradition
depending on scribes who did not know a word of
Romance. But at least nine are clear enough to warrant
translating on their own.

What ever can I do? What's to become of me? My dearest one,
Do not forsake me!

My lord and master Ibrahim, sweetest of all names!
Come to me, in the night –
If you won't, if you don't want to, I'll come to you:
Just tell me where to meet you.

Tell me, how can I bear this separation any longer?
This poor loving girl has only eyes for you!

I'll love you, I'll love you all you want – but only on
                                        one condition:
That you swing my anklets right up to my earrings!

No lover boy will do for me,
Except the dark-skinned one.

Mamma! How I do love the blond boy
With his little neck so white, and mouth so red!

Oh Mamma, my lover is leaving me, never to return –
What can I do, Mamma? He's leaving without even a kiss!

The Watcher wants to keep me away
From the one I love, who loves me too;
Just because he belongs to someone else!.

At the dawn, the very dawn, of this St John's Day feast[57]
I'll put on my best embroidered gown –
And break a spear to pieces![58]

Notes

◆

1 This line contains an untranslatable play on words between *nur* (light) and *nuwwar* (flowers).

2 Twelve silver *dirhams* (cf. *drachma*) equalled one gold *dinar* (cf. *denarius*).

3 A reference to the *Ka'ba*, the Holy of Holies in the Great Mosque at Mecca.

4 'Magus' refers to a Zoroastrian, a follower of the dominant religion in Persia before the Arab conquest.

5 The reference is to Joshua stopping the sun from setting. The poet here plays with the old formulas of Arab love poetry.

6 This enigmatic reference may be to Quran 15:24 and 29:39, where Haman and Qarun join Pharaoh in opposing Moses and are punished by flood and fire; see Professor Corriente's notes to this poem in *Twenty-Seven Muwashshahaat and One Zajal by Ibn al-'Arabi of Murcia (1165–1240)* (ed. Corriente and Emery, London and Zaragoza, 2004).

7 Entry by Vicente Catarino in *Medieval Iberia, an Encyclopedia,* ed. E. Michael Gerli (London, 2003).

8 The great translator of Arabic and Persian poetry, Anthony Arberry, gives a beautiful translation of this in his *The Ring of the Dove* (London, 1994), p. 16.

9 Low-hanging fruit: this is a reference to a verse in the Koran where the fruits of Paradise are so described.

10 This is another reference to the *Medinat Al-Zahra* royal pleasure gardens of Córdoba, which were the wonder of the world at the time of Ibn Zaidun and Wallada.

11 *Sidra*: tree of Paradise; *Kawthar*: river of Heaven; *Zaqqum*: bitter-fruited tree of Hell; *Ghisliin*: pus which exudes from the pores of the damned in Hell.

12 This famous poem (translated in part) begins with the formulaic invocation of life-giving rain on the beloved's former campsite, more appropriate to Arabia where it originated than to Iberia; but the depth of feeling the poet shows towards his native Córdoba more than compensates.

13 This is the Moorish palace, standing where the Bishops' Palace does now; not the present (fourteenth-century) Alcázar de los Reyes Cristianos.

14 The editor of the *Diwan*, Bustani, says that '*Nabi*' (Prophet) is a place in Córdoba; I have not been able to find any evidence of such a place, and interpret it as referring to the time rather than the place.

15 Rusafa: a famous eighth-century lodge and garden north of Córdoba, where the first Umayyad ruler of Spain, Abd al-Rahman I, planted palms and other Syrian plants to remind him of his native land.

16 This poem was written from prison, after the poet had spent five hundred days there.

17 This 'holy water' is *ma' at-tasnim*, a daring reference to mixing wine with the drink of the blessed in Paradise; in the previous verse, there is a reference to a Koranic verse as well (sealed in musk); see also the poem by Ibn Zakur.

18 'wine' here is *sulaf*, the choicest wine made by juice obtained without pressing the grapes, presumably from over-ripe grapes.

19 This long stanzaic poem – of which I have translated only part – is my personal favourite of all Andalusian love-poems: uncannily melodious, speaking of heartfelt personal passion and disappoint-ment, evoking his beloved Córdoba, past its prime but still 'be-guiling'. This is, incidentally, a rare example of a poem that satisfies

all classical Arabic criteria for great poetry (canonical structure, thematic progression, skilful – and copious – use of rhetorical devices and perfect versification) as well as Western ones (personal feeling, musicality, economy).

20 Ibn Bajja's client is an Almoravid, one of the warlike Berber tribe who came to help the Andalusians against the Christian advance, and (predictably) took power for themselves; the Almoravid men wore veils . . .

21 'Almoravid joy' pops up in zajal 68, line 9. The Almoravids (a puritanical North African tribe who ruled al-Andalus during Ibn Quzman's lifetime) were not known to be especially fun-loving. 'Wrapped up' is a reference to the veils Almoravid men wore.

22 Another rather ordinary stanza of praise.

23 Clouds and rain are a stock-image of plenitude and satisfaction in Arabic poetry.

24 This line is in Romance: *Todo ben kireyo*, 'I desire all that is good'.

25 Literally for *fatir* (Arabic for leavened bread) and *labta* (Romance for unleavened bread)'.

26 'Laleima' if a name, it is indeed an unusual one; but none of the corrections proposed encourage me to override a clear graphy in the text.

27 The last word in this line has generated a lot of controversy. I follow Sr Corriente in relating 'shilibatu' to *sibilare/ '(re)chiflado'*.

28 Presumably opposite ends of Córdoba. There has also been a lot of argument over this verse.

29 A triple pun, on Thurayya (proper name, metaphor for wine, and the constellation the Pleiades).

30 All words in italics are in Romance in the original. Many of them have been variously interpreted, for there are very few other sources for Romance at this period; but '*Vino! Vino!*' is as clear as can be and would have the desired result if shouted today in the right parts of Córdoba.

31 *volcón* : Romance for 'pouring, draught'.

32 Inventor of wine . . .

33 Sr Corriente interprets this as a dialogue between the poet and his penis; this is corroborated by the injunction in the stanza after next.

34 The last three lines are full of Romance words, even in the rhyme. Some are obscure, with the exception of *qardhaj* (*cardo*, 'thistle') and *igranon* (*grañón*, 'porridge').

35 This has to be one of Ibn Quzman's greatest poems: no pandering to a powerful rustic, no cheap humour or easy pathos, just what appears to be an old man's heartfelt reflection on love, life and ageing, with a lyrical transition from despair to (almost) jollity to deep melancholy that will stand any comparison I am aware of. That is why I have tried to give some faint impression of the movement of the poem, by leaving the stanzas unrhymed and fluid, the refrains with their choppy internal rhymes.

36 This *zajal* is ostensibly in the 'tradition' of the ribald iconoclast Ibn Quzman.

37 I.e. the sacred Black Stone of the Ka'ba in Mecca.

38 Ma' as-Sama': see the next note. The Sevillean royal line ending with al-Mu'tamid was more properly known as the 'Abbadids (banu 'Abbad).

39 This is an untranslatable play on the name of the 'Abbadid tribe (*banu Ma' as-Sama'*, literally Sons of the Water of Heaven, the latter being a proper name).

40 In case the reader has not guessed, this poem is not about love, but about a walnut.

41 God was said to have split the moon as a portent of Muhammad's prophetic mission. This is a rather daring image.

42 This verse contains an untranslatable, multiple play on words, the root of the words for 'fawn or gazelle', 'weave', and 'amorous thoughts or verse' being the same . . .

43 See Robert Irwin's splendid book, *The Alhambra* (London: Profile Books, 2004), if you want to distinguish the few known facts from the many fanciful legends.

44 See the biographical note to Ibn Faraj, above.

45 A play on words, to 'coo' and 'prose' having the same trilateral root.

46 Another (trite) play on words, '*nawr*' meaning flowers, and '*nur*' (same consonants) meaning light.

47 The Sabika is the hill of the Alhambra and Generalife.

48 Wadi Munajjim: a rich oasis in Saudi Arabia; but this would make more sense if it were in Granada, and I have a suspicion this reference might explain the hotly debated etymology of a town and river near there, known today as Monachil; in any case the image is a (self-conscious) play on words, *munajjim* meaning 'astrologer' and 'astronomer' . . .

49 Another pun: *burj* means 'tower' and 'constellation'.

50 One theory – perhaps supported by this verse – about the name 'Lindaraxa' is that it is a contraction of '*ain dar 'Aisha* ('the eye of Aisha's house'), Aisha being a wife of the king.

51 Anyone interested in reading more women's verse from al-Andalus, and who reads Spanish or Arabic, should consult *Poetisas arábigo-andaluzas*, ed. Mahmud Sobh (Diputación provincial de Granada, *c.*1985).

52 Male palms grow a cone-like protuberance with pollen, which must be manually applied to the female palm (unless the birds do it). Wallada resented Ibn Zaidun's apparent bisexual tendencies (see the next fragment).

53 Mary and palm-tree: Mary was said to have taken refuge near a palm-tree; see Quran 19:22–23. The name 'Wallada' means 'giving birth'.

54 Abu Bakr shares his name with the first Orthodox Caliph who succeeded to the leadership of the community after the death of the Prophet Muhammad.

55 Professor Sobh thought this last line was Romance 'Cuán marrano',
   but the term *marrano* (from Arabic *muharram* or 'unclean, forbidden',
   applied to New Christians forcibly converted from Judaism) is much
   later, offends the metre and anyway the Arabic verse given in the
   manuscript is perfectly clear.
56 The Andalusians wore white for mourning.
57 The *'Ansara* fell on the 24th of June (St John's Day) and was a
   midsummer feast celebrated by both Christians and Moslems.
58 The text and literal translation of this line is clear; but the meaning is
   not. Professor Federico Corriente (whose selection and text I have
   followed) thinks it is a sexual allusion, but unfortunately does not
   interpret it for us.

Index of First Lines

How many nights I spent, nights woven of your dark hair 24

I beg you to entrust to me a parchment 108
I can see a garden, with ripe fruit to be picked 110
I fritter away my life in drink and debauchery 66
I have a lover, who's stubborn as can be 99
I have often shied away from a forward, willing girl 36
I miss my lover so, and yearn for him night and day – 99
I never saw nor did I hear of a pearl 32
I once saw a black man, swimming in a pool 26
I spent the night beside the riverbank, close by her 76
Ibn Zaidun, famous as he may be, reproaches me –
    blameless as I am! 101
I'd give my father for a gazelle from distant Hima, one
    guarded by a 57
I'd give my father for the one who leaves me weak 104
If my sacrifices meant anything to you, don't heed those who
    blame me 54
If only you had eyes to see with whom you speak 103
I'll love you, I'll love you all you want – but on one condition 112
I'm bored with Seville, and Seville is bored with me 54
In the heat of battle, I recalled Suleima, and how I felt the day we
    said goodbye 18
It was perfect, when she came to call: we spent a night of bliss 84

Just as the night came trailing its dusky train 19
Just look at Ahmad, untouchable in his glory 19

Laughing through pearls 53
Leave wealth to those who care about it 54
Leave your problem to Fate – that's kinder to the soul 27
Love resides in the rising of these stars 50

Mamma! How I do love the blond boy 113

May the rain-clouds grace the loved one's campsite with
     their bounty 48
Memories kept me sleepless, of a faraway, lost home 23
My beloved came to me, and did my bidding – 73
My eyes may not be full of tears, but that should not
     make them say 19
My friends, it's not heresy to love your sons 83
My lord and master Ibrahim, sweetest of all names! 112
My love for you is without blemish 39
My lover's house, now he is gone 70
My master has taken power, and tyrannises me – if only 82
My tears disclosed my secrets by the river, for its beauty 109

No lover boy will do for me 112
Now do I yearn for you, Laleima, little star 64
Now that we've separated, what hope is there for us? 100

Of all the local girls, I chose her as my queen – 21
Oh, God! How beautiful is the garden of youth – 92
Oh horseman, riding like the wind 108
Oh Mamma, my lover is leaving me, never to return – 113
Oh Wallada! Your secret's out, your baby's born 102
Oh, you who have a thousand lovers, and loved ones 103
Oh, you who pine for Nejd, sighing for it all the time – 90
Oh, you who severed the cord of my affection 47
Oh Zaynab, wife, if you have ridden far away 60
On the morning of our parting, we brought our horses
     to a halt 28

Pass round the cups of crimson-lipped wine 95
Pass the cups here in the dew-damp meadow 84
Pouring tears, burning heart 54

Quite drunk, she stretched full out and fell asleep 30

Separation has dawned, replacing our closeness – 41
She brings me my wine in her lovely little hand 32
She came to me in a dream, in a blessed, lonely place 88
She came to me like the reddest rose 72
She has a rump, such a fine substantial rump! 31
She has the eyes of a gazelle, the neck of a doe, wine-dark lips 25
She sighed, and my passion's flames were fanned 84
She stood there, shielding my eyes from the sun's bright disk 76
So you think you are the world's best judge of beauty 107
Stuck without a drop of wine: now what could be worse
     than that? 66

Take this pittance from the hand of a captive; if it contents you 80
Tell me, how can I bear this separation any longer? 112
The bird of sleep thought my eye was a nest fit for him 60
The brightest night of all, I'd say, was when 18
The gossips did their best to come between us 109
The heavens weep, from evening rain-clouds and
     from morning ones 78
The love I feel for you, by definition cannot end – 39
The night we shared was sent to us, a raven-haired harbinger 20
The pennants of morning are unfurled 89
The radish is a splendid food, but the mouth 69
The spreading Earth is like a buxom young girl 29
The sun came close to the moon: wine, and a friend
     to drink it with! 82
The sword has in its heart a stream 30
The very air would seem enamoured of my love 29
The Watcher wants to keep me away 113
The West Wind caressed me with its gentle breath 51

The wood reveals the secrets of the garden, the river 25
The wound in his fair cheek is no accident – 84
They ask me, 'Can you love this gap-toothed one?' 33
They looked upon her eyes, and entered passion's trance – 31
They reproached me, blamed and castigated me, for loving one
   like him 85
They said 'Your hair's gone grey!', and I said 34
Those tawny cheeks were so light and bright 17

Wait for me, I'll come to you as soon as darkness falls 100
What ever can I do? What's to become of me? My dearest one 112
What I love: the taste of wine 61
What would it hurt you to feel pity for me 50
When will I be able to tell you how I feel? 48
Who will rid me of this stupid suitor 104
With the dawn came a vision, so clearly revealed 37
Wrapped in a double cowl, as pretty as can be – 81

You see before you one well-used to faithfulness 80
You were once the most elegant of men 107
You who treat your friends with gifts of peaches 102
Your new-growing beard has written on your cheek 32
You're like a willow, when your long, thick tresses stir 23

Index of Poets